MOVING IN

A Moving Thought

I have been through so much - but look at me still standing strong. I could write a book about my life and it could be made into a movie. Never have used it for anybody to pity or to think I want their love – I am strong. I am beautiful because I have survived more than you could ever know... And through it all I still find the courage to love, never damaged from the past.

A Woman's Guide to

Moving in the *Right* Direction

Surefire Strategies for a Happier, Healthier and Resilient Mindset

Ella Patterson

Bestselling author of 1001 Reasons to Think Positive

You cannot change your destination overnight.
But you can change your direction.

\- Jim Rohn

Also by Bestselling Author Ella Patterson

1001 Reasons to Think Positive
Will the Real Women Please Stand Up!
Will the Real Men Please Stand Up!
Pampering Pleasures
Heated Pleasures
Sexual Healing

Coming Soon

The Chameleons
It Is What It Is
A Woman's Worth
Pick a Better Partner
The Dirty Red Game
Successful Things That Successful People Do
Stupid Things Men Should Never Say To Women
Higher Expectations
Life Lines
Life Lessons
Life Goes On
Celebrations
Smart Moves
For The Sake of Women
The Potent Woman
Relationship Quickies

KNOWLEDGE CONCEPTS PUBLISHING
Texas Oklahoma Arkansas Missouri Illinois Tennessee

A Woman's Guide to

Moving in the *Right* Direction

For information regarding special discounts for bulk purchases
Please contact Knowledge Concepts Special Sales:
P.O. Box 973 - Cedar Hill, TX 75104-0973
or call 972-854-1824
or email us at kcespublisher@aol.com

Moving in the Right Direction
Ella Patterson -1st. Edition
p. cm.
1. Women. 2. Self-Help. 3. Motivation. 4. Self-Improvement. 5. Psychology.
I. Patterson, Ella. II. Title.

ISBN: 978-1-884331-33-5 CIP: 95-94105
LCCN: 2006923877 SAN: 257-6163

This book includes an index
Manufactured in the United States of America

10 9 8 7 6 5 4 3 2 1
Library of Congress Cataloging in Publication Data

U.S. $14.95
CAN. $18.95

Praise for
A Woman's Guide to
Moving in the Right Direction

"Ella Patterson has a unique, yet realistic and down to earth way of conveying the intricacies of living life to the fullest. Having served as her pastor, I am proud to see her share words of living a complete life to a hungry generation."

- Pastor Frederick D. Haynes III,
Pastor, Dallas, Texas

"Moving in the Direction will awaken you from your nap of complacency and compel you to see and hear your own life anew – with all its fullness of possibility. With wisdom and honesty, author Ella Patterson shows us that the recipe for true success takes determination, strength and spiritual tenacity."

- Retired Lt. Commander
Herbert L. Jones Jr.
U.S. Navy, Atlanta, Georgia

"Moving in the Right Direction delivers on its promise. It's inspiring, motivating and packed with strategies that really work. It moves you to take the proper action so that you can transform your life."

- Tom Joyner
Worldwide Radio Personality

"Finally, a book that's really designed to uplift women. It touched all of my emotions- it was very moving for me. Thank you for touching my soul."

- Denella Richard
Travel Specialist

To my beloved grandmother, Annie Mae Owens,
who taught me how to drop to my knees when praying.
and showed me how to live as my authentic self every day.

To my mother, Elizabeth Branch Jones,
for her extraordinary gift of life and living
and who had one of the strongest mindsets I ever seen.

To the 2.9 billion women of the world.

Contents

A Woman's Guide to

Moving in the *Right* Direction

An Overview

My life now is all I've ever needed, but it hasn't always been what I wanted. Growing up, I wanted to do things the right way, so I made choices that would create my vision of what I thought was my perfect image. After the disentanglement of each of those attempts, I found myself broken, scrapes and bruises on my body, scars on my heart, and eventually falling apart until finally I surrendered to my knees in prayer. I came to understand the only way I could stop traveling the wrong paths and making bad decisions was to create a book of collective efforts that would consistently move me in a better direction.

The writing of this book has been a beautiful transformation, even though sometimes difficult for me personally. I am so grateful for the opportunity to do the work that I am called to do – encouraging women to live more fulfilling lives.

In the pages that follow are powerful strategies that you can use for building a lifestyle that will make you happier, healthier, and provide you with a more resilient mindset.

I want to share my story with you. I think that sharing my journey will allow you to open your mind to the possibilities that life can be better. Somewhere along the way you will recognize yourself and your own experiences of traveling the wrong path. And my hope is that whatever refinement I've tasted and whatever knowledge I've gained can now be passed on to you. My story is not always attractive, but I think that you'll agree parts of it are beautiful. The parts where God reminds me who I am and what I am destined to do. There are moments when my faith has been tested and then there are times when God sees me as His daughter traveling on a divine course fulfilling my own destiny. At times I'm sure He sees you in the same way.

Because each of us has a strong need to improve in some area of our lives this book is designed to help you discover the "you" who you've always wanted to be. It is an undertaking that would not have been possible without the help from many gifted individuals, so as you read I would like you to keep in mind that this is not a book that you simply read and hope that by reading it you will move in the right direction. This is the kind of book that you *must do* if it is to work for you. By *'doing'* this book your life will change for the better. You will become naturally happier, healthier, and more resilient. This is my promise to you.

Tweet me your comments @emp55

Now let's get started!

Introduction

When Life is filled with Crisis

You'll have to live life in order to get through life.

Gaining Knowledge and Understanding

There I was sitting in the middle of my dining room floor; crying and full of fear. Ten years ago my life took a turn for the worst. Everything I owned was being sold or placed in foreclosure. My bank accounts were being closed, my publishing company was being reorganized, my manager was being sued, my book editor had been fired and I didn't know what action to take or what direction to go. Someone had dropped the ball in my life. My career was on hold. There were no new book projects planned and to top things off I had gained fifty pounds - which I wasn't trying to lose. Things weren't looking good for me. I was officially in the dumps and deeply depressed.

A few months later I found myself filing for Chapter 13 bankruptcy and suddenly my list of negatives had grown. My father was placed in a retirement home, my mom was diagnosed with diabetes, my friends and colleagues had dropped from my 'closeness list' faster than I could count to five - and many of my dearest relationships had fallen apart.

So, here I was; ten years after signing my first seven-figure major book deal, I was out of work, out of money, deeply depressed and ready to throw in the towel. I kept thinking to myself "how can I fix my mess?"

I had worked since I was fourteen years old, but now I was out of work and emotionally lost for the first time in my life. I didn't know what to do with myself. I felt empty and trying to find the energy to change my state of mind was difficult. The only thoughts I was thinking were negative. I was lost. My life was in crisis mode and it didn't seem to be moving toward change.

Little did I know - that out of my depressive state and negative happenings my greatest positives were about to come. It was now ten years later and I had been given a chance to make things right. The opportunity to move forward was staring me in my face and it had come in the midst of much personal pain, pressure and pitfalls. I could finally see the light at the end of tunnel. I was being given another chance. Doors that were once closed had begun to open and time had begun to heal me.

The one thing that was always consistent in my life was my ability to write. I had always loved to write no matter how bad things got for me I kept producing manuscript after manuscript. I would complete one book and then began on another one. My life had a way of changing for the better when I did what I loved.

Even when my life was spiraling out of control writing was a simple pleasure I enjoyed. I felt good in bad times when I was writing. So today, I am pleased that many doors have opened for this book to land in the hands of people from all walks of life. I have seen, heard and experienced this realization every single day since it has been written. There isn't a goal you cannot accomplish with the right mindset. It doesn't matter who you are, how old you are, or where you live: this movement is stronger than you.

I hope that by sharing my stories along with those of other courageous people you'll find the inspiration and strength to take those first steps you need to get whatever you want in life. Many amazing experiences and success stories are featured in this book. They come from all over the world, yet they work for one common purpose: to move in a direction that is beneficial - and right for you. Included are easy paths, tips and shortcuts that I have learned.

As you experience this book and its words and you begin to learn - you will also come to have, be, and do anything you want. You will come to know who, what, and how you can move progressively forward in life. You will also come to know the true beauty of those things that await you.

Now, let's fast forward a few years. It took some time, but I finally overcame my shame, self-pity, and downward spiral. I was tired of feeling sorry for myself so I picked myself up and got back to doing what I love most … writing! I officially decided to start my life over.

To restart my writing career I began publishing small manuals for the business travel industry. I contacted a few premier hotels and resorts; pitched my empowerment manuals, featured their resort or hotel on the front cover, sent them samples, interviewed with them and began to earn some much needed income. I also invested time into travel writing. I did this for more reasons than money. It was the thing that made me smile and boy oh boy did I need to smile.

While visiting one of my assigned travel destinations I was approached by a young lady named Paula who was also a professional travel writer. I shared a few details about my writing ventures with her and she asked me, "With all the writing you've did why haven't you written about the automotive industry?"

I didn't know where this question was coming from, so I asked her why such a question. She went on to explain to me that after she met me on yesterday she googled my name and noticed that I had written several books and how-to articles. She went on to say that I should try my hand at writing automotive review articles.

After talking a little more with her, I asked her for a few contacts and she gave me the name of a guy in Texas, where I was living. I reached out to him over the phone, Federal Expressed him my press portfolio as he requested, and by the next week I was test-driving brand new vehicles. My cars had been repossessed, so this was a blessing in disguise.

Regaining Your Life

It was challenging, but to date, I've written fifty-two new books, self-published eight, published a local consumer newspaper, hosted five flourishing web sites, and I'm currently writing my next three books simultaneously.

I'm now back in size 12 clothing, reasonably in shape for a 58 year old woman, and I'm happily speaking to women of all ages about having higher expectations so that they can steadily move in the right directions. How did this happen? It's a question I've asked myself often, but my answer is simple. It was because I never stopped trying. I never gave up, nor did I give in. I never stopped believing. I created my new life by taking baby steps.

Regaining my life was slow at first, but I worked on improving small parts of it each day that I woke up. I made a list of things that I should do and then I followed through on my list one task at a time. I prayed for strength, peace of mind, and prosperity daily. As I tackled one task I crossed it from my list and then added another new task.

As I worked to regain momentum I could feel my situation beginning to change. I was finally moving forward. Yes it was slow, but it was steady. Of course there have been a few bad decisions along the way, but I've learned that all mistakes are not bad mistakes, so when I do make a mistakes, I quickly correct them. Once it's corrected I pick myself up and forge ahead remembering the goals I'm trying to reach. I now understand why I must learn from my mistakes.

When I think back it's funny that I've always said I did it myself. I've always took pride in doing things myself. But doing things by myself had a double edged sword in a strange kind of way. Not delegating has had its ups and downs. It's not that I couldn't get someone else to do it; I just felt that if I did it, it would get done faster. So, when I speak of writing and self-publishing books, I think of it as doing it myself, one day and one struggle at a time. I crawled like a baby, back to what I know - back to writing for women who need help with getting to where they want to be. I love doing this!

Have you ever had chaos, confusion, disorder, uproar, mayhem or turmoil in your life? Have you ever felt like giving up and throwing in the towel? Have you ever felt as though life has thrown you a curve ball and you can't hit a homerun? Maybe you've been guilty of eating until it hurts. Maybe you thought this was the best way to hide your pain and you hated yourself the whole time you were doing it? How many times have you ignored your problems by trying to run from them?

Have you ever looked at your life, your family, or your home and felt sorry for yourself? Have you ever felt like your life was not your own anymore? Did it feel like your life belonged to someone else, and it was just on loan to you? If you have felt any of the emotions mentioned you were certainly having a moment of crisis. Most of us at one time or another has experienced crisis.

During those turbulent days of my own crisis I recall that my book publisher was moving slowly to renew my contract, yet I was being told that "You are so encompassing, just write and we'll do the rest." So, I kept writing and thinking that everything was okay. Then my editor got pregnant, married, and fired all in that order. Timing was not working in my favor and I didn't know what to do. I was feeling a bit out of sync because I had never experienced this kind of turmoil. I had never been paid seven figures either. Back then I had a team of knowledgeable people assisting me and I still managed to lose everything that I had worked so hard for.

In the past as long as I was doing things for myself everything was going smoothly. As soon as I turned my business ventures over to new people turmoil started creeping in from all directions. My crisis was professional, but yours could easily be a personal or professional crisis. The discomfort and defeat feels the same. Whatever pains you're going through in life, remember it's the curve balls of life that throw you into a tailspin. When you're blindsided and don't see it coming, you don't know how to handle it and when it hits you you're caught off balance.

The good news is - you don't have to stay down and out. You can change the direction that your life is going. You may not be able to change everything or make someone love you, but you can learn to love yourself better. You can live a life that's worth living and you can gain love for and control of your own life.

Don't think so? Neither did my friend Sheryl, who was hit by a stray bullet and is now paralyzed from the waist down. Neither did my aunt Leana, who was diagnosed with breast cancer, or, my mother Liz who was raped by a drunken teen, or my friend Debra's whose marriage was a sham and soon fell apart, or my friend Betty who lost everything in a real estate scandal, or another friend named Stephanie whose husband committed suicide and Carol whose husband went to jail for seven years and when he was released he left her for another woman.

I couldn't believe that so many people I knew had gone through these kinds of disappointments. Each of these people has learned how to pick themselves up and move forward in the midst of great personal turmoil. I applaud each of them. They have become my role models.

There have been other great people in the world - some are no longer here with us, but while alive they were strong and determined to make powerful strides in life. They showed us every day that we can win; even in the midst of great defeat and turmoil. Maybe you know some of these people. The people I speak of are Oprah Winfrey, Hillary Clinton, Gladys Knight, Barbara Streisand, Princess Diana, Helen Keller, Mother Teresa, Marian Anderson, Rosa Parks, Jane Adams, Susan B Anthony, Sandra Day O'Conner, Jennifer Hudson and even Brittany Spears are proof that we can rise in the face of defeat.

I asked myself why more people don’t know how to pick themselves up, and get back to having the kind of life they really want. A burning desire to share what I discovered consumed me – so, I began to search for more people who had once been shattered and broken, but have learned how to pick up the pieces and put their lives back together. I looked for people who have found a way to heal, and now have great self-worth.

As I began to seek out and speak with people I soon discovered that one-by-one people began to emerge and as they did I gained knowledge about how they became engulfed with hope and determination. As I worked on repairing my own life, one helpful person after another began to come into my life. When I discovered one person who had picked themselves up, another would come. Every day another person who succeeded appeared. It was as if they were all linked to one another in some kind of way. If I was riding in my car, at the grocery store, taking an airplane, or walking in a mall they all seemed to form a beautiful chain that possessed similar knowledge and understanding.

If I began to lose focus or my concentration diminished or I went the wrong way, somehow I would meet wonderful people who helped guide me back on the right path. People whom I didn't even know were there - trying to help me. There was a presence of this wonderful force trying to offer direction and support so that I could travel the path I was meant to travel. Now I knew that the universe was on my side. I could feel it working in my favor.

If I felt like I was on a lone journey, something or someone would come into my life and help me understand my plight. It felt as though I had a private guide by my side to keep me going in the right direction. If I entered names in the Instagram search engine it would lead me to a site where I discovered more wonderful people who had also struggled and then succeeded. I envisioned telling the world about what I discovered and how this discovery has helped change my life. I am pleased to play it forward and help you move forward in your life.

A Moving Thought
The journey of one thousand miles begins with a single step.
- Chinese Proverb

Chapter 1

Moving: One Step at a Time

"We learn who we really are and then we live with the decision"
- Eleanor Roosevelt

Proceed With Fulfilling Changes

L**et's rewind for a moment**. The year was 1998. I was going through a wonderful transformation. I had earned my first million and I was happy, successful, and full of hope for my future; then a friend of mine asked me who would take over my business if anything ever happened to me. This got me thinking. I hoped this wasn't a question in need of an imminent answer...but I thought about it, and then replied, "It would be nice if my children took over my businesses." If I died I would want my children; who are grown now, to keep my legacy alive and I hoped my children would use some of my written works to move them forward. This is what I would like, but I have to remember that they have their own lives to live and if they are happy doing what they do that's good enough for me.

I ask you, my readers this same question. "Who would take the reins and move your name forward into history. Who would you delegate or hope would help your name live on?" What if there was no one. Could you say that you have taken the proper steps to keep your legacy alive? If not, what could you do today to set that act into motion? I decided after long thought that I should do something about my own legacy. How about you?

So, here I am writing this particular book, and for all intent and purposes it's my comeback project, my resurrection, a way to help others get out of their rut and get back on track.

My Life Story Tells This Story

Not long ago the success I gained when I wrote my first three books seemed to disappear slowly. I recall everyone trying to get something from me. One by one their hands were out, and little did they know that all the handouts had finally taken a toll on my bank accounts. I was dying financially, but I wasn't going to let my weakness take me hostage. My bank accounts were drained, but I was still alive and determined to regain normalcy in my life. I would regain my life step by step, one task at a time and if this plan worked then maybe I could use what I learned to help someone get pass their problems in order to live a better life. But there was a bigger problem.

I did not have any idea of how I was going to mass-produce this phenomenon. I had to think deeply, so with determination and faith I flew to one of my favorite destinations to be alone. I cleared my appointment book, dug in, took no calls and began writing. When I felt that I had wrote enough about what I knew I flew back home and found more people to help me bring this book to life. One year later I had everyone in place to help this dream come true. With over 1600 hours of meetings, working my butt off, hundreds of phone calls, interviews, and many discussions I used my life story to tell this story. Another year later you're holding a book that you can use your own life and work.

I used what I knew about moving in the right direction to create Moving in the Right Direction. Wonderful people were attracted from everywhere. The right people were drawn to me and before long Moving in the Right Direction was completed. Six months after completion it was published. As this book took on a life of its own, stories of how life was changing for the better for people who came to us. People wrote about finding their dream job or succeeding in home based businesses, believing in themselves, having confidence again, and being better and becoming more productive in their careers and personal lives.

A Process of Small Significant Changes

With help from this book people are rededicating and recommitting themselves on jobs, in relationships, and in life. With this commitment you can let go of past failures and grab hold of belief again. You can work toward your goals and when you get tired; you can sit and rest for a while. Working toward a new you is much the same. You can get back on your feet and journey toward a world of success. It's a process filled with small significant changes. Just like a turtle, you can move slowly and cautiously, but like a turtle you can only move forward when you stick your head out. And it's the same in life. We can all move in the right direction, step-by-step, little by little until we have reached our goals.

Bringing Fulfillment in Your Life

We have received accounts of how Moving in the Right Direction is being used to bring fulfillment in people's lives and how their lives have improved in many areas from having a better understanding with their life partner, to earning large sums of money, getting new cars, better jobs and promotions. Businesses and relationships are transformed within days of applying the strategies of Moving in the Right Direction.

There have been uplifting stories of relationships with family and friends being reestablished to happiness. Some of the finest stories have come from people who are best friends and found themselves in the midst of turmoil, but after using Moving in the Right Direction their lives were transformed and they found the stimulus to forgive and love again.

There are moving in the right direction get-togethers being held all over the world as people share the knowledge with their loved ones, families and friends. I have also been impressed by the numerous amounts of people and businesses that have incorporated moving in the right directions into their book club readings.

All of this has taken place in only a few months after writing this book. I have spoken with many of these people. It's amazing the happiness I have been able to witness.

What Kind of Book Is This?

As I stated earlier, this is the kind of book that you *must do* if it is to work for you. This is not a book that you simply read and hope that by reading it you will move in the right direction. The strategies in this book are for people who are seeking to improve their lifestyle. It will help you draw upon your personal power.

Because this is meant to be a positive book, some chapters have been made super short so that you can read them, put this book down, practice the techniques, and then go back to where you stopped reading. It gives you incredible insight that offers long-term successes.

Let's be honest, each of us has a strong need to improve in some area of our lives. Our quality of life often reflects how we handle our day-to-day tasks. One of the greatest opportunities you can have is a chance to finally move from a negative place to one where you can start over - gaining control of the most important asset you have. YOU! Any improvements you decide to make will ultimately move you in a meaningful direction, but first, you must start the process. Change begins one gesture, one person and one step at a time.

How This Movement Helped Me

I think it's important for me to speak about why having a Moving in the Right Direction mindset is worthy of an entire book. I came across the idea one day while looking back over my own life.

Over the last forty-five years, I've had an opportunity to study the mindsets and principles that motivated me as a young girl. I didn't know it then, but one day in June, as a young girl, I decided if I was going to continuously move forward in my life I would have to make consistent improvements.

Before I could improve my life I had to think better of myself. I had to have a sense of moving in the right direction so that I could take action right away. To keep from spiraling out of control I had to develop a plan of action that would last. You see, I learned very early in life that if we took the proper action we could overcome many obstacles that plagued and weighed me and other people down. This book is perfect for that.

How This Journey Will Help You

I hope by now you know whether or not you want to take this journey - to move in the right direction and become a better you! Before you begin I would like to suggest ways you can effectively receive the most from this material.

It is designed to be your life long companion. It has suggestions at the end of each chapter that will help you focus on moving forward when you are ready.

As you steadily progress, and begin to understand and implement Moving in the Right Direction you can go back time-and-time again to the strategies to expand your knowledge, skills, beliefs, and desires.

Become a Student

Instead of being a student who is learning for the first time - become a teacher. Take an *"I'm going to move-in-the-right-direction approach*" and read with a purpose in mind. Learn, share, and discuss very soon after you read it. Spread the word and implementation will become second nature. Knowing that you will be teaching these practical principles to someone you care about will make an important difference in your learning experience. It will make an impressive difference in your life too. Try it now as you reflect back on what you've already read.

Integrate the Principles of This Book

In addition, as you share what you're learning with others, you may be surprised to find that negative perceptions that others have of you may soon disappear. Those who listen to you will see you as a changing growing, positive person, and will be more inclined to help and support you as you work to achieve your goals. Perhaps together you can integrate the strategies of moving in the right direction into your lives.

Once you realize that no one can persuade you to change and that you are the only one who has the ability to change *you*, only then can you really understand and live the principles in this book.

Only then can you encourage others to improve. I am comfortable telling you that noticeable - positive things will happen for you.

It doesn't matter what bad things others say about you or think of you, you will care more about helping them think better of themselves, their lives, and their relationships. You'll no longer allow other people's opinion to guide your life or weaken you. You'll find it easier to implement personal change because there is more within you that is essentially renewed.

This Is Not a Quick Fix

This book is not meant to fool you into thinking that it's a quick fix. But I assure you; you will feel the benefits and see immediate payoffs. It is this clearness that gives everything its value. Heaven only knows how to put the proper price on its goods - "You." Get involved in more ways than one. Shape it and indulge it in your own creative way.

Moving in the Right Direction is a wonderful celebration that creates new life in us! It serves as a tool to help us celebrate every aspect of our lives. Here you'll acknowledge some universal goals that we all strive for: a great career, financial freedom, a loving and attentive soul mate, a healthier body, caring friends and family, time for self, peace of mind and a way to make this world a better place to live.

Embark on this truly remarkable experience and use it, learn from it, experiment with it, and grow because of it. It's an exciting road map of useful lists and things you can do that will help you gain control of the ways you invest your time, energy and talents.

When It Begins To Work, Tell Others About It

As it begins to work for you tell others about it. Any change or improvement in you has to begin with ***you***. It's one of the most important features for winning in life and helps you become better in your personal and professional world. Play it forward by telling someone.

Helping You Follow This Book

To help with each chapter; take the checklists and implement them with what you already know. Then watch how you begin to improve in most all areas of your life. Here's what I suggest:

1. Find a comfortable place to read, somewhere quiet and motivating - a place that you consider your space. Here, you should be able to abandon inhibitions and be creative with your own inventive nature.

2. Read this book alone at first. Allow each improvement to unfold, naturally. Include your own ideas as you advance your knowledge. I've reserved space in the back of this book for notes.
3. Reading this book from cover to cover is best, but if you like, you can dip in different chapters or sections for helpful hints whenever the mood strikes.
4. Let go of any negative feelings or complications about your past mistakes or problems. Take deep breaths often, then inhale and exhale slowly to release any anxiety you're feeling.
5. Understand that you don't have to perform rigid tasks in order to gain your new perspectives.
6. As you read, select and then circle at least twenty new ways you can live the life you desire. Then try to create a few more of your own. Again, use the spaces in the back of the book or use your Movement Journal to jot them down.

Slow Down and Take Your Time

Like others you may choose to read this book in one sitting because it gives good direction, however, I recommend you slow down and take time to savor and digest each strategy. This will allow you time to incorporate *Moving in the Right Direction* into your life - one step at a time.

A Moving Thought

"Most great people have attained their greatest success one step beyond their greatest failure."

~ Napoleon Hill

Chapter 2

Mindset 1

Achieving an Extraordinary Life

In this chapter you will learn that all things change into one another. Past pains can help you change into your true self.

Putting Your Plan to Work

My **future as a young girl didn't look good**, but I've always had high expectations. I suppose some of you who are reading this book might have experienced the same feelings. Most of what we believe about ourselves came from our past hurts and disappointments in life. "We know who we are, but we don't know what we may become." We need a better perspective of who we are, and who we may become.

In my case; who I was brings to mind some difficult years as a child. There are two incidents in particular. As a young girl I recall that there were attempts from a grown male cousin to molest me. His name was Tichey (he was 30 and I was 7 years old when it began). He tried to molest me at least ten times, succeeding one of those times. I was 14 years old when he finally touched me with his private part. I became so afraid to trust men because I felt that if a family member would try this, no one is to be trusted. Years ago as I watched the movie - The Color Purple, in the scene where Sophia who was played by Oprah says, *"Girl child ain't safe in a family of men."* It reminded me of my own childhood drama.

I Remember Running

I remember running to hide under my bed, under piles of clothes, inside the clothes dryer, and again running until I was out of breath to get away from him. I never told a soul. I was afraid until I became a grown woman. I was twenty eight years old, married, and pregnant by my husband when I finally told my mother about his many attempts to molest me. And the reason I told her then, was because I was angry at her. I had held my feelings inside for twenty one years before I ever breathed a word of it to anyone. I blamed my mom for not protecting me from him. She worked during the day and it was during summer days that Tichey would visit our home, around 12:00 noon.

He drove a city transit bus and every time I heard the air brakes from the bus that he drove, I would run and hide. He walked through our home looking under tables, beds and behind curtains trying to find me. I remember hiding under my bed one day and all I could see were his feet walking around my bedroom looking for me. I could see his fat feet moving and raising from the floor as he squatted to look under my bed.

As a child I never felt safe or trust toward any male figure. I always thought there was a motive if they offered me the smallest gift, so I ran.

Why I Blamed My Mom

Tichey always had a pocket full of coins. He gave my brothers coins that he took from the bus. You see, there was a small confectionary store that sold candy down the street from our home and that allowed him enough time to be alone with me and attempt to molest me. This went on for eight years. I ran for eight years too, until he finally caught me.

The truth of the matter is he was able to get to me because my parents trusted him to check on us kids while they were at work. He would check on us kids each day that his bus route took him past our house. I believe that I blamed my mom because he was her cousin. I grew up blaming her for my fears and hatred toward adult men.

And Then…. I Apologized

I understand why children who are molested or abused yet they don't and won't tell. Fear is overwhelming and as a child, how do you explain your turmoil without losing your mind? Every time I would get the courage to tell I would mentally and physically shut down. My whole body would freeze and my mind would go blank. I did not know how to handle the pressure.

I was only seven years old when it started and he would threaten to tell my mom that I did it to him. And guess what … a kid who is afraid will definitely believe that she is the blame. Some days I thought my mom was in on it because after all she was the one who sent him to check on us.

I began to play it in my mind that she had sent him to our home knowing that he was a molester. I thought she told him to have freedoms with me even though deep down inside I knew she didn't. To blame her was the easiest way to deal with the horror of this terrible memory. I later apologized for blaming her.

I Barely Knew this Lady

Another pivotal time in my life as a child that I recall is when I was sent to live with a lady I barely knew and to this day I still don't know why I was removed from my home and placed with her. I recall that day as if it were today. My mother told me to go to Ms. Geneva's house after school. I thought I was going over there to wait for my mom to pick me up, but my wait lasted for more than six months.

While living with Ms. Geneva, it never felt like home. It felt more like a boarding school, so one day, after six long months I decided to leave. I woke up early, got ready for school like normal, all the while thinking of home. My mind was made up, I was going back home. The weird thing is, once I got back home, I never felt like I belonged there anymore. It stuck with me that I was uprooted and moved to Ms. Geneva's home. The day I returned home was the day I began to live as a loner within my family. I never felt quite the same. I felt that family love for me was less.

The Child Molester Died

Now, let's fast-forward twenty three years later. My mom told me a few years after I informed her about the molestation attempts the molester had fell dead in front of his home. Once I knew that he had died I started working on forgiving him, but I have never forgotten the little girl who ran for cover when the big bad bus with the loud airbrakes came to the house.

So now, here I am after all those terrible moments in my life, living a better life today than I ever imagined. I have used my desire to become successful as a means of catapulting me past the pain and degradation.

So, Now I Know Better

Maybe your situation is different from mine – maybe you never had to worry about molestation or anything so drastic, but I want you to know that you're not alone in your difficult situations. If you have experienced any kind of fear and pain I want you to use this book to get you to a better place in your mind, your life and in your profession. I know that you were born with the potential to overcome any obstacle just as you were born to live an extraordinary life.

I didn't know it back then, but now I know better. I never would have thought when I was a young girl being molested by my mother's first cousin that I would go on to become a successful educator, earn more than seven figures as a published author, host motivational seminars or teach women the importance of loving themselves in the purest ways.

Turmoil and Crisis Happens

Every day I find myself talking to a friend or family member who's gone through some kind of drama that's causing them an increasing amount of stress. Little do they know that their pain and stress is causing them to remain stuck in a place that they so desperately want to move away from. They are either going through employment crisis, family disaster, financial problems, job difficulties, relationship turmoil or social pitfalls. Devastation and turmoil can happen to any one of us, at any time. The truth is… it can happen more than once too.

Had The Universe Turned Against Me?

Now let's fast forward to the newest past, just a few years ago, I was going through the most devastating time of my life. My car had been repossessed, I owed money to every bill collector in town, and my father was suffering from Alzheimer's. Now, he had been admitted into a retirement home.

To top that off my mother had gone through a triple by-pass operation and one of my cousins was choosing to live in poverty. My oldest brother had lost his life-long job with the navy, and one of my younger brothers had died of a massive heart attack a few months earlier. All of this family turmoil was driving me crazy and making me worry excessively.

My business and personal relationships were in turmoil too and I had worried myself into high blood pressure. My life was a total mess. It felt as if the universe had turned against me.

I Had To Go Through It

Little did I know that out of my greatest gloom I would be given a chance to get my life in order. I remember praying every night and often during the day. I asked God to place his hands on me and wrap his arms around me. This was my prayer. This was my song every day. Then one day I noticed that things in my life were changing. God had shined his light on me and after a full night of meditation and prayer I began to do something about my situation. I had begun my own personal improvement plan. I was suddenly in the midst of a positive movement. I could feel and see my life changing right before my eyes. I began to witness good things happening to me and I was finally coming out of the storm. I did not know exactly how I was going to tell the world about this powerful movement, but I had to go through it before I could fully understand it and I had to understand it before I could tell anyone about it.

Don't Be Afraid of Change

If we have, but one guarantee, it is that change is inevitable. You can't be afraid to change what needs to change. It is happening all around us and because of this ever-constant change we learn to attract people, places and things that are good for us and will help us. Change is good for us and many times it's the best thing for us.

One of my personal moments of change reminds me of a time when I was a freshman in college. I was offered an opportunity to own my own gymnastic studio. At the time I was teaching in a National Youth Sports Program, a program that encourages youth to actively participate in sports during summer months.

I worked as a Gymnastics Coordinator for the past two years and upon a visit from Washington by one of the national officers my work was observed and documented as exceptional. I was offered a chance to own my own gymnastics studio, but because I had never been exposed to such opportunities, I was afraid to take the offer. I was afraid of change.

The Start of the Life You Desire Lies Within

My upbringing had taught me to be fearful of people that offer gifts for no apparent reason. I was afraid to accept rewards for my excellence or rewards that I honestly earned.

I say this to tell you that no matter what your circumstances are, what hardships you've experienced, or what turmoil is in your life the answers you need in order to live the kind of life you desire … lie within you. You have all that you need to succeed, but you have to dig inside of yourself and bring it forth.

Today You Can Begin Again

Sometimes the rewards are handed to you on a silver platter, but you might fail to realize it because you lack confidence to believe that you are worthy of such gifts. Whatever has happened in your past; whatever wrongs you have encountered and whatever mistakes you have made are over. Today we began with today. Today you can wipe your slate clean. Today you begin to understand that nothing in your past matters at this moment.

Today you accept the rewards that you earn and those that are due to you. Your decision to start new sets you free to decide that you will get past your mistakes, hurts and pains. And guess what… you will do it because you can do it, and you deserve it because of all the things you have already gone through. Your movement begins today. Your time is now!

You Are Destined For an Extraordinary Life

Because you've began reading this book you're undoubtedly interested in learning something about moving forward and making some positive changes of your own. As you begin moving forward learning, discovering and embarking on new ways to do you, you'll start moving forward in your life too. You'll discover that the act of moving forward affects everything you desire to do in your life.

Simply taking these first steps opens doors for all kinds of possibilities. To access the answers to your own questions and live a happier life - you have to start your forward movement today. Don't be afraid. You're on your journey to improve your life so start where you are. Begin today moving toward a life that is right for you.

Change Is Natural When Tailored to You

Positive forward movement encourages us to do what we have to do to succeed. It is such an important tool that it helps us determine the power of transition, and transformation. It helps us take a truthful look at ourselves and how we view our lives. If we use change to effectively move us in the right direction it can help create opportunities that help us live the way we want rather than settling for whatever comes our way.

Change is possible. It comes more easily and natural when it is tailored to our own unique gifts, experiences and passions. Get physically and mentally connected and passionate about your dreams and you'll be able to make the following commitments without hesitation.

1. I will change my life?
2. I will enhance my sense of belonging?
3. I will create more time for myself?
4. I will take better care of my health.
5. I will find ways to reduce stress and create balance in my life?
6. I will work to have peace of mind in my life.
7. I will live my dreams.
8. I will become committed to living the kind of life that I desire.
9. I will no longer allow the past to control my present or my future.

Get a Head Start on Your New Beginning

Whether you are a corporate executive working fifty hours a week, a single parent trying to raise a family, a young adult whose trying to find your place in society, a woman whose been abused, or someone who's overworked and tired of feeling stressed and pressed for time; there are choices about how to move toward a life that you can love. All you have to do is step back, look at where you are in comparison to where you want to be, and then reevaluate your priorities so that you can make conscious decisions about the kind of future you'd like to create.

Right here is where you began to listen to your life because only when you truly listen will you gain the insight to start doing the things you need to do to get a head start on your new beginning.

Listen to Your Inner Voice

Once you've made the commitment to make the proper changes all you have to do is listen closely and you will hear your inner voice speaking to you; telling you what's best to do.

When you are curious and honest enough to answer important questions - you begin to grow. You've probably asked yourself ... "How do I start anew?" "How do I make the best decisions?" "Where can I turn once I've decided to improve my quality of life?" These are questions that need to be answered even though it may be difficult at first.

Because your life is full of learned skills - you possess the tools needed to make positive changes. Because you've never listened closely you probably assume it is complex or difficult, but it simply means focusing your attention on things you've experienced that steer you in the best possible direction - toward the unique path of your life's highest potential.

Let me explain further … when you are willing to listen to your life it means you are also willing to develop powerful relationships. Your mindsets starts with God, yourself and the people you care about as well as strangers you encounter. Listening closely helps you gain direction for finding and staying on the right path. It's the art of listening that helps you create the kind of vision that unlocks doors and creates wonderful successes and learning experiences. When you listen to what your inner voice is saying you are able to tap into your confidence to believe that even when it seems nothing is coming together the way you hoped you have the tenacity to flow smoothly through the twists and turns of life. Those things that threaten to knock you off your course are less bothersome now. Having the power to listen opens you up to the possibility of receiving rich and abundant rewards to live without fear. When you listen to your inner voice you'll hear the personal storm coming before it is upon you. Your instincts are sharpened. It is this kind of listening that allows you to prepare before you actually fall.

Here are five important motivators that I would like you to remember while listening to your inner voice:

- First, give yourself permission to move forward. That's the only way you're going to be able to make positive adjustments in your life.

- Second, ask yourself what you want from life and then listen to your inner voice. It knows what you really want. It will give you the best answers. Carefully listen with your heart, mind, body and soul. The answers will come.

- Third, embrace what you hear and then put what you learn to good use.

- Fourth, once you have learned what to do....DO IT! It's your time. If you want to improve your life you have to get off your butt and move toward what it is that you want.

- Fifth, put fear behind you and reach for your goals.

Hopefully any mishaps, mistakes, hardships or heartaches you've experienced have given you enormous insight and propelled you forward on your journey. Hopefully, a journey that's positive, beneficial and rewarding with insight to understand that you must go through it in order to get through it.

We Each Are Very Similar In Many Aspects

Like most people, each of us has worked diligently to move in a positive direction in order to gain success. Like others, I used almost every skill I have and tried many jobs. As a matter of fact, I've held so many jobs that I felt like the jack-of-all-trades and master of none.

People want to feel successful in all that they attempt to do and isn't that what we all want - to feel successful at what we do so that we can use our success to help others and help ourselves?

We want what really matters to us.

I no longer desire the corner office, but I would like to have a healthy bank account. I no longer live to see my name in lights, but I do live to light the way for others. I no longer think about me, me, and me; instead I find ways that I can assist others as they move their lives in the right direction. My mission has changed and my goals have been updated. I strive to help others live their dreams and along the way I hope to live a few of mine.

I Was Born To Do, What About You?

I'm strongly convinced that I was born 'to do.' With that in mind, I changed my thinking and my approach to fulfill my tasks. Now my mission is to simply succeed. I don't bother with those bothersome things that have no real meaning or substance. I accept no new manuscripts from want-to-be authors who don't understand the mindsets needed to complete the tasks or get the job done. I now have an office manager who helps prioritize my calls; a property manager to manage my real estate properties, and I stepped away for a restorative three months so that I could complete my work on this book.

You are now holding in your hands the results of that effort - something I hope will help you move forward in your own life.

I'm not going to pretend that living in a big house and driving nice cars isn't my idea of grand, but what really makes my life worthwhile is the experiences that have gotten me to this wonderful place in my life – and in this place I can definitely say I have begun to appreciate the things I love and the people I care for. I relish life and my soul appreciates who I am as a person. The designer clothes I wear adorn a size 12 body that I respect and have grown to love!"

Continue Your Work and Help Others

My business is my life's mission and I love what I'm able to do to help people who want to succeed in life, love and the workplace. Even more important than all of this is the fact that my friends genuinely care for me and feel that I am a loyal friend to them. My

22-year-old grandson and my 19 year-old granddaughter thinks that I'm cool. This year they even bought me a T-shirt that says, “This is what a cool grandma looks like.” My husband of more than thirty five years considers me his favorite person in the world and still says I make him laugh. I am a child of God that still has a lot of work to do before I'm done on this earth.

So, from this day forward when you help people achieve their goals and they don't show appreciation, simply chalk it up as a worthwhile lesson learned about people. Become more determined than ever to continue your life work of helping others reach their personal goals. As you read can’t you see much of who I am in yourself? We are all in some way or another like each other.

What I Believe

I believe that success is gauged by one's interpretation of personal fulfillment and satisfaction. There is no *one size fits all* explanation.’ Success is individual, subjective and versatile, or at least it should be, but what makes life's journey worthwhile is that each of us has common desires. We want security, money in the bank, good health, caring friends, supportive family members, a good life and peace of mind.

We truly can have all of the things we want in life. I believe this now and I believed it when I was very young girl. Even when I was an innocent child being chased by an abusive relative I could see the light at the end of the tunnel. And as an adult when I was standing in line filing for Chapter 13 Bankruptcy, I could hear a little voice whispering in my ear... saying to me *"This too shall pass, this too shall pass."* And guess what? It did!

I am a better woman for having gone through those experiences. I didn't know it then, but as sure as my name is Ella Patterson, I know it now. There is no one left to blame. I would never want to go through it again, but I know that I'm stronger, wiser and smarter all at the same time for having gone through it.

What I've Learned

I've learned a lot since those times and I understand why I had to go through loosing almost everything in order to get to this wonderful place in my life. My desire to be a winner in life has helped me come from behind and end up out front. What I have now and what I had before is that I am *not* a victim of my circumstances.

I am a person with the power and fortitude to ride out the wave and weather the storms of life. Now I can rise above pain and difficulty knowing without a shadow of doubt that joy and peace is mine. If obstacles present themselves, I step around them. If opportunities don't present themselves I find a way to create them.

If you have this same mentality, and I suspect you do, you can move forward and overcome your problems too. No matter how big or small the problem you can move in the right direction. Not in the direction your siblings have moved, not in the direction your parents have moved, not in the direction your best friend has moved; but in the direction that is best for you. In a direction that makes you want to dance and shout to the world from the highest mountain, *"I am living a life of my own choosing and I love my life!" "I feel like I am really moving in the right direction."* Take all of the mistakes you've made and then turn them into worthwhile lessons by understanding why you made the mistakes in the first place. Learn the lesson my friend, learn the lesson.

Moving Toward Your Goals

The most popular question I get from people is, *"How do you get so many things done successfully?"* My answer is simple; "Don't do a lot of things, only do those things that move you in the direction that will help you get closer to your desired goals." Learn to say no to those things you aren't passionate about, and minimized the time you spend with people who drain you. Try your best to surround yourself with people who believe in you and are willing to support your efforts.

Make time to nurture and rejuvenate yourself so that you can continue to do the critical work that's needed to catapult you toward happiness and peace of mind. When you do too much you lose focus and almost everything that you've worked hard to get. Don't do like I did because in the past I was my own worst enemy!

Understanding Your Own Possibilities

As you begin to understand how setting goals can become beneficial for living the life you want you will also learn the importance of choosing the right path. Anything is possible when you move toward the right path. You can find growth and peace of mind, not as an escape from life into protected inactivity, but find it as powerful center of energy in order to find your happiness.

You can find successful living, not as a means to fame, fortune or power, but as a practical application in life to achieve worthwhile goals.

Understanding your possibilities teaches the joy of renewal and a disciplinary way of life - a life that offers personal fulfillment as you achieve victory over self and the difficult circumstances of the world by doing what's right.

Two Key Prerequisites for Success

The best part of my career has been spent in the field of education and I have worked long hours discovering how some people soar to fantastic degrees of success while others who have equal qualifications and more experience move aimlessly through life -- never achieving the noteworthy things they truly desire.

Many people have the qualifications needed to succeed, but they don't know how to use those qualifications to achieve personal success. There are two key prerequisites for success:

- Determination and
- Perseverance

These same factors are associated with failure when there is a lack of the two. `Let's dig deeper into why some people succeed and some don't.

Attributes of Successful People

In Anthony Robbins book, Awaken the Giant Within, he states, "*I've questioned many successful people - asking them to identify personal attributes and characteristics that have helped them develop. They agree that their principles are basic, definite, specific, transferable and easy to use.*" These same people have similar traits in common:

- They make lists and follow through on the lists.
- They have a thirst for taking action, so they take action.
- They work consistently to get things done.
- They don't procrastinate.

Wherever successful people assemble - these powerful traits are evident and noticeable - and are found in people who are often in charge of the meetings. Successful people are usually very confident and because of their outward determination others may assume that success comes without effort to them. Nothing is further from the truth. They are delicate people, people who can be harmed by insensitive words or actions - no matter how unintentional. Just because they work hard and find creative ways to take action does not mean that they don't have feelings.

Attract What You Want

Everything that is coming into your life is being attracted by you. Good or bad you are the magnet. It's attracted to you by the images you hold in your mind. Attraction is forever in action, just like your thoughts. Wise people know this.

When you focus on the things that you want over and over again, you get what you want. When you focus on the things that you don't want over and over again, you are attracting what you don't want. If you want positive things to happen in your life, simply start thinking about the positive things that you want, and then do something every day that moves you toward getting what you want. Your entire life is a physical expression of what you are thinking. We all tend to acquire confidence and personal success -- one project, one success and one thought at a time.

To gain your success start with thinking about what you want and as you begin to think notice the positive things that slowly begin to happen. Notice how your positive thinking will bring your success closer to you.

Life Is Full of Trials and Tribulations

Since life is filled with trials and tribulations we will have to fail sometimes before we can learn the lesson.

That reminds me of a story I read a few years ago: Thomas Edison's laboratory was virtually destroyed by fire in 1813. Although the damage exceeded two million dollars, the buildings were only insured for a little over $238,000 because they were made of concrete and thought to be fireproof. Much of Edison's life's work went up in enormous fire and flames that night.

At the height of the fire, Edison's son, Charles, desperately searched for his father among smoke and debris. He finally found him, calmly watching the scene, his face glowing in the reflection, his white hair blowing in the wind.

"My heart ached for him said Charles," He was 62 - no longer a young man - and everything he owned was going up in flames. When Edison saw his son he shouted, "Where's your mother?" When he told his father he didn't know, he said, "Find her. Bring her here. She will never see anything like this again for as long as she lives." The next morning, Edison looked at the ruins and said, "Thank God we can start anew." Three weeks later after the fire, Edison managed to deliver his first phonograph.

We learn from the trials and tribulations that we experience and sometimes we gain great success from these pains and pitfalls. Many failures are not bad, even though they may feel like they are. Most people, no matter who they are - have times when their lives are out of control, unmanageable, chaotic, and filled with drama, What about you? Ask and answer the following questions.

1. **Question:** Has your life ever been so out of control that you felt nothing you did was right? Explain.

   Your Answer: ______________________________

   ____

2. **Question:** Have you found yourself daydreaming about things that you would like to accomplish, but haven't?

Your Answer: ______________________________

____

3. **Question:** Have you found yourself stretched in too many directions by the demands of others? Explain.

   Your Answer: ______________________________

   ____

4. **Question:** Have you found yourself becoming tired and ready to give up on your personal, family or job duties?

   Your Answer: ______________________________

   ____

5. **Question:** Have you ever felt like getting out of bed would be a waste of time? Explain.

   Your Answer: ______________________________

   ____

6. **Question:** Have you found yourself not knowing which way to turn - to make things right again? Explain.

   Your Answer: ______________________________

   ____

In our pursuit to succeed it is sometimes difficult to accomplish the goals that are most meaningful to us. With *Moving in the Right Direction* you can start today - changing your life, living your dreams and achieving your most desired goals.

Decide Where You Want To Be

Set a time line for where you want to be thirty days, six months or a year from now. Decide what it is that you want from your life. Decide where you want to be, and then start working on the best plan to get there. I don't want to sound mean but *"If you don't know what you want, how do you expect to get what you want?"*

The Bumpy Ride Syndrome

As with any commitment you'll bumpy rides from time to time, and that's okay because most all successful people go through a few bumps in life. They refer to this bumpy ride syndrome as "learning through experience." Precious resources of time and energy will be used while going through it, but don't fret; the ride and your efforts will be well worth it.

Imagine a speed bump in the road. Life has little speed bumps too. Our speed bumps of life are there to slow us down. Sometimes we don't want to slow down, but life knows what's best for us

Take Small Steps at First

When you're hurting and feeling overwhelmed by events that have taken place, it's very difficult to imagine putting yourself at more risk. It's difficult to stick your neck out and take chances, but think of all the chances the poor turtle takes.

Should you safely hide in your shell never moving forward and never making strides or gains in life? Is it best to sit there and never come out until it is safe to move along. No, that's not the best thing to do. You can wait it out, letting the world pass you by never living or doing anything worthwhile, but I assume that that's not what you are made of. I suspect when it comes to you --- you are a go getter, a vibrant person who wants to live your life to the fullest. Why don't you take small steps at first until you feel safe and are ready to take bigger, bolder steps toward your success? That's the first step to moving in the right direction. It's easy when you are resolving to come back from disaster to set lofty goals for yourself. Don't do it. Save the big goals for later. You can save the world in due time. For now, just aim for getting back to being you.

How You Can Finally Move in the Right Direction

Ask yourself…"What can I do to move me and my life in the right direction?" Here are few important mindsets to remember.

- Decide how long you want to take before reaching your goals.
- Set your goals in a thoughtful, reasonable manner. This way you are guaranteed to get great results.

- Establish goals to sort out the challenges confronting you.
- Prioritize the areas and activities that concern you most.
- Don't be afraid to make adjustments. Flexibility is a tremendous factor in having the power to change. You might have to change your timeline or adjust it to meet the demands of your time.
- Take a realistic look at your goals. This lends balance along with knowledge and insight on how to use your resources in more meaningful ways.
- Have more than you desire. Having the desire to live your life to its fullest is great, but desire alone is not enough. To lack desire means to lack one of the key ingredients to achieving success. Many a talented individual failed because they lacked desire. Many victories have been snatched by the underdog because they wanted it more. So, if you desire – intensely - and you act upon it, everything stands within your reach.

It's important that these steps be used to excel you -- so that you are able to enjoy the beauty and rewards of life.

You've got to think about big things while you're doing small things, so that all the small things go in the right direction.

\- Alvin Toffler

A Moving Thought

"I will look for purpose every day and in doing so I will find the love in my heart that enables me to love being who I am, and show love to the people I care for."

Chapter 3

Mindset 2

It's Time for Change

In this chapter you will learn how to move in the direction that will help you gain success and happiness.

In Life Everything Must Change

We're going through some wonderful changes at our house. We finally cut the apron strings and let each of our children soar. So look out world, whether you're ready or not here they come.

Right now my daughters are in their 'let us soar on our own' stage. This is where they very seldom take my advice because they already know everything. At least that's what they think, but every time they take on a new adventure they have to call and let me know everything they experienced. Minds are going, thoughts are spurting and eyes are big as door knobs. They get so excited when they speak to me now-a-days.

Any day now my daughters will need me again and forget that they are grown and come running back to mommy again, but until then I'm letting them exercise their wings and feel their own power as independent women. They'll experience life, stumble a few times, maybe even fall, and hopefully they'll pick themselves back up and then keep moving forward.

Change Helps You Move Forward

How badly do you want to get to a place in your life where you are comfortable with who you are and what you have? Are you willing to do whatever it takes for the chance to live entirely on your own terms? Is it an all-consuming feeling that you can't quite understand? Do you stay awake at night dreaming and wishing you could change the way things are progressing in your life? If so, you're lucky. You're lucky because you live in an age of enormous opportunity for anyone with enough desire to get to a higher place in life. I should know since my dreams and persistence began that way.

An unknown author makes the point that *"Knowing how to move forward is good, but knowing how to move in the right direction makes a big difference."*

So it's safe to say that you can move in a positive, safe, rewarding and successful direction if you work hard at it.

No matter how old you are, your gender, or marital status; your desire to move in a direction that's beneficial and right will definitely make a difference in how quickly you succeed.

As with the turtle that can only move forward when he sticks his head out - so do we. We are similar, but in order for us to move forward we have to sometimes stick our necks out. So as you stick your neck out and make forward moving - steady progress you might stumble and fall sometimes or even meet head on with roadblocks but you have to keep taking more steps. You have to make changes and keep moving forward, one step at a time.

And as I sat at my desk and watched old videos of my ever-growing daughters move toward their freedom – I found myself reflecting on what I'd just said to T'Juanna, my youngest daughter. "You can only move forward in life when you stick your neck out." If you don't stick your neck out, you can't experience the changes needed to move forward.

And so it's the same mindset for life.

When we feel overwhelmed by life's ups and downs, or when some kind of personal pain has taken place, it's very difficult to put yourself at more risks. It's hard to stick your neck out.

But think of the rewards.

Take a step for yourself - move in a direction that helps you reach your goals whether they are small or insignificant. It's easy to think you are ready to move forward when you are resolving to make a comeback from a disaster. It's easy to set lofty goals for yourself. DON'T! Save your big goals for later. Let's just work on saving you now and then we'll save the world. For now get yourself in the right mindset to take on the goals that you already have. Aim for reaching one goal at a time.

Have a Passionate Adventure

The search for something more becomes a passionate adventure, one that will provide you with all the amusing anecdotes, profound turning points, and provocative choices you'll need to live a life without regrets. True adventure starts with an inclination and desire to enter the unknown. It is with this desire you hope to find more of yourself or of the universe. It is with this desire you learn to bite the bullet, stick your head out and move forward in life. It is with this desire you hope to find more of yourself. You hope to move in a direction that your choices are conscious everyday so that you can shed "the old" - old issues, old problems, old drama, old rivalries, old anger, old resentments, and old pains.

We have no business in this day and age to wallow in what caused us pain or held us back…this is the emotional baggage we are supposed to be getting rid of.

This is a choice you must make if you want to take your life to the next level. It requires a point of departure, the willingness to shed what's predictable in order to embrace the new people, places, passions and predictabilities. Make this your most passionate adventure.

What Are Your Expectations?

I'll let you in on a secret. In the past when I was going through my turmoil, my only goal was to get my butt out of bed. My second goal was to simply take a shower and brush my teeth. Then one day after long thought my mindset changed and I decided that I was going.to take my life back. I was going to own me again. I resolved to make a real change. So, from that day forward, I decided to get myself moving. I listed every single dream I had on a piece of paper, and then I went to the nearest office supply store and bought me a journal just for my dreams. I carried it everywhere I went. It was the small handy purse size-kind. I looked at it every day so that I could stay on track.

Some days went well, than some days dragged with no real signs of progress. On some days it was very difficult for me to reach even my smallest goal. It's like that sometimes. But no matter what I still tried.

I discovered that because my mind said change; did not mean that change was going to happen. The situations that brought you to your lowest point will still exist. While you've resolved to take small steps to reach your goals the big problem that's made your life so complicated still exists. Those are the times you might get discouraged and slow down or give up. Then again, maybe you're afraid to confront the real demon. Maybe you think that it's not time yet. How many times have any of us made commitments to do something and by the end of the week we've forgotten the plan. Take baby steps and keep your pace slow and steady until you fell that you are ready to pick up the pace.

You Got To Live Your Life

I still feel weak to my knees when I think of my children moving out and moving on. I remember when my oldest daughter, Juanna decided to play professional football. At one of her games she took an illegal hit and her knee was shattered. If only I were there I could have helped. I cringe at the fact that I wasn't there to help her during this painful time. It's been a constant reminder that I can't there to protect them all the time. I realized that I had to live my life and allow my kids to live theirs so that I could keep my own dreams alive.

When I was going through my own turmoil I knew I had to pick up and keep my life moving forward. No one will do it for me. I had to allow my children to live their lives and I had to live mine. Nobody was going to turn my life around, except me. My baby steps had to include a support system other than my husband.

My goal was to simply get out of bed every day and do something to improve the life that I was living. Once I got out of bed I would try to turn on my computer and complete my manuscripts. If I became good at that then I would make plans to do something else like, maybe going out of the house or just sitting in my yard from time to time. It was a slow process, but things started getting back to normal.

I attended writer's classes, seminars and spoke with other female professionals that had the same or similar interests as me. The women were so positive, upbeat and willing to make changes in their lives. This let me know that I had to get rid of my pity party moments and find renewed energy. I needed to put the energy that I had been wasting into something that I loved to do. As I did this I slowly began to feel my spirit change and my energy level rose to new heights. I began looking forward to waking up and doing things that empowered me. I kept my goals low and my focus intense. I was on my journey to recovery, feeling better and stronger as each day passed. I was able to take on tasks and challenges that were so difficult to do and seemed impossible before. I can't believe that I picked myself up and was able to regroup without falling apart. No one could have told me that I was going to make a comeback.

Live The Life That's Waiting on You

A lot of people are unwilling to step out and work toward their goals because of personal fears. The truth is we must be willing to get rid of the life we've planned, so that we can have the life that is waiting for us. We have two choices between two unknown worlds when we are trying to move in the right direction; one world tempts us by making us think "what a dream to live like that! And the other world is placed before us to stifle us and hold us back. It's simple when you expect more and do more you get more.

Little Choices Count Too

What if I told you that one month from now you could be living your dreams, but every day between now and then you would have to choose your destiny. In other words that there is at least 30 other choices standing between your dream and whether or not it is to come true.

You'd probably say that's all, only thirty choices. That doesn't mean big choices either. Little choices do count. The little choices we make have a tendency to alter life too. Whether you chose to walk away from an argument, channel your anger, wash a load of clothes, empty the dishwasher, tune out by meditating, watch your favorite movie, eat your favorite dessert, drink a refreshing cold drink, or call your best friend to catch upon things.

Trust and believe the tiny choices happening day in and day out can literally shape your destiny just as much as doing something big or elaborate. True life is lived to the fullest when tiny choices are made. Tiny choices bring about tiny changes. But with any change the smallest and minutest change on a regular basis with consistency really makes the biggest improvements in your life.

Some people might use the excuse that things are changing so why try anything risky. We must all remember that life is always changing and success can be attained by anyone who wants it and is willing to work hard to get it. With passion and a little sweat you can have anything you want.

Five years ago I was a woman who was striving to build my business and had great determination to build a high profile and fulfilling brand. Today I have completed many of my goals, but as each day arrives I set new goals that will help me reach bigger goals. You should too.

Work At It as You Work For It

Think about it, there are billions of people in the world, and there's one thing that every one of us has – personal expectations. The good news is you don't have to buy them. The other news - not necessarily bad - is that you should want to move in a direction that works for you, a positive direction that improves your quality of life and enables you to accomplish your dreams. It's not something you can just sit around and wait on, you have to work for it and also work at it.

Ask yourself the following questions and then answer them.

1. What is it that I want from my life?

   ____

   ____

   ____

2. What would make me feel successful?

   ____

   ____

   ____

3. How can I accomplish my goals in the least amount of time without taking short cuts that would harm my efforts?

    ____

    ____

    ____

4. How can I be the best person that I can for my family, job, and myself?"

    ____

    ____

    ____

Consider that it is not always easy to become successful and remain successful? In fact, to most people it's hard, but if you keep working at it; in the end, it is a beneficial journey filled with joy, hope and victory.

Ask For Guidance

I recall the day I sat down and began writing this book. I knew that my best work required more ability than I possessed and therefore, I needed the kind of spiritual help that only God could give. I had to also gain a working partnership with people who believed in my activities and supported me. I suggest you find a great support team too.

I had a very earnest session of prayer, asking God for guidance, and that I am allowed to put this difficult project into powerful hands. As I worked on my manuscript I often relied on my faith and prayers to help me through it.

When this manuscript was finally ready for publication I prayed … dedicating it to God. I asked only that this book would help people find ways to live successful and happier lives. I thanked God for his help and dedicated the book once again. After prayer, I took it to my editor, made the necessary changes and then headed to my printer. After delivery to my printer I felt a sense of accomplishment. I now knew where I was going.

Do You Know Where You're Going?

Let's pause here for a moment, and figure out where you want to go in life. From the words of Mark Twain, "*Not all horses are born equal. A few are born to win*" Like me, maybe you are compelled to start your life over from scratch. In the Bible's book of Revelation, either death or divorce or debt or disaster gallops into our lives, and suddenly our familiar world comes to an abrupt end. If we should lose our health, home, partner, job, or we have lost our way we must start over from scratch.

"Starting from scratch", is a familiar saying, but do we know where it comes from. Not from the kitchen while baking, but from the rules of the English horse racing, which permitted gentlemen to fix races so that in theory all the horses could cross the finish line together, with the winner only beating his competition by a nose. This never happened, but creating the illusion of a great showing the horse that was considered the finest runner was sent back and had to start the race from behind a line scratched in the turf or the gravel.

In modern horse racing the fastest horse was weighted down with heavier saddle bags in order to equalize the competition. Incredibly the more races a horse wins the more weight he had to carry. There are wonderful stories about Secretariat – arguably the century's greatest thoroughbred - leaving other horses in the dust along with dust in their nostrils. Not only did he finish the race as a winner with fourteen pounds of lead bars as he sped across the finish line not by a nose but by a thirty one length lead.

After this wonderful horse died, an autopsy was performed and it was discovered that Secretariat had an enlarged heart. His heart was larger than any of the other horses, and many claim that he won races because his heart was larger than any other horse. It was believed that because of his heart he only lived to fulfill his natural destiny. I don't know if this is true but the biggest question behind Secretariat is was he born with an enlarged heart or did he grow a large heart in order to live up to his destiny?

Secretariat knew where he was headed each time he began the race. Do you know where you are headed? If you have an idea of where you're going you can began to move in a direction that's right enough for you to get where you're trying to go.

When You Don't Change

I'm sure you have felt the pressure to sometimes do too much. You might even get a little anxious sometimes because you may not know what it is you want in life. Of course it's frustrating sometimes - to the point of throwing up your hands and giving up. Not knowing what you want or how to go about getting it can send you tearing off in the wrong direction.

Believe me, you're not the only person who thinks this way. We have all asked ourselves "What should I do with my life?" I think that's the major reason the world is full of so many unhappy people. They know they have great potential, but tragically they have not taken the time to figure out what they want to do. They have not created a vision of what they want for themselves. It's not that they don't want to change; they just can't imagine how to change or what to change into. They don't know how to get from the "how-do-I-do-it" to the "how-I-did-it."

Eventually, you may recognize that you are on the wrong road, that you are going nowhere fast; and because of pride you refuse to pull over to study your road map. You refuse to change your mind - so the directions you're taking can lead to nowhere.

Change Is Good and Beneficial

You should understand that it's okay to change directions in your life. Change is good, but while trying to change you might find yourself going from one thing to another, never thinking to take inventory of your personal abilities and capabilities. You might discover that you don't take the necessary time to find out where you really want to go, what you really want to do, or what your deepest desires are. Then as time goes by you have no true sense of direction so you get frustrated and become angry. Now your attitude toward people is changing and your own goals began to get overwhelming. So by now you start to blame others for your pitfalls and lack of accomplishments.

To most people goals have great meaning and it's what they are taught to want in life, but first –

- What is it that you want?
- What is it that you expect?
- Where are you going?

You need to know these three things before you can ever reach your desired goals. This reminds me of a story that I heard about Pete Rose. I've never met him, but what I heard has taught me a valuable lesson that has changed my life. Perhaps this same story can help you.

Pete was being interviewed in spring training the year he was about to break Ty Cobb's all-time hits record in baseball. One reporter blurted out, "Pete you only need 78 hits to break the record. How many at-bats do you think you'll need to get the 78 hits? Without hesitation, Pete just stared at the reporter and very matter-of-factly said, "78." The reporter yelled back, "Ah come on Pete, you don't expect to get 78 hits in 78 at-bats do you?" Mr. Rose calmly shared his philosophy with the throngs of reporters who were anxiously awaiting his reply to seemingly boastful claim. "Every time I step up at the plate, I expect to get a hit! If I don't expect to get a hit, I have no right to step into the batter's box in the first place!" "If I go hoping to get a hit," he continued," then I probably don't have a prayer to get a hit. It is this positive expectation that has gotten me all of the hits in the first place."

To this day when I think of Pete Rose's philosophy and how it applies to my everyday life, I feel a little embarrassed. As a writer and motivational speaker I was hoping to convince people that belief is powerful. As a mother, I was hoping to be good mother. As a married woman I was hoping to be a good wife.

The truth is that I was an adequate motivational speaker, a good mother, and was an okay wife. I immediately decided that being okay was not enough! I wanted to be a great motivational speaker, a great mother and a great wife. I have changed my attitude to one of positive expectations, and the results have been amazing. Because I changed my thoughts I have become fortunate enough to secure a great book deal as a writer. My son thinks that I am the best mother in the world. And my relationship with my husband is enduring, loving and attentive and that's more than enough for me. Thanks for the lesson Mr. Rose!

Are You Stuck?

So many of us are in similar positions; we want to get more out of life and from life, but we don't know how to go about getting it. Simply put, we don't know how to unlock the doors. As a whole most people don't know how to do what they need to do to change. They are unhappy and unsatisfied because they feel stuck. They don't know what to do, so they don't move at all, they remain stuck. It's as if their life is on pause.

Imagine you're receiving great respect, admiration and status. You've got everything that everyone else thinks they want to have. But, all of your success is keeping you stuck in your present position. All of which makes it difficult for you to ask;

"Is this what I really want?"

"Am I going in the direction I want to go?"

Of course some people have a great life; it's all they want and all they need in order to feel satisfied. And that's great if this makes them happy, but what if they are just going through the motions and working every day on a job they are not satisfied with? What if this same job is offering them great amounts of money, yet it is not fulfilling. The question: Are they rich and unfulfilled? Are they stuck?

Finding Your Balance

Then there are others who appear to be successful, yet they can't find happiness or balance in their personal life or careers. They need more to make them happy. They want to find ways to achieve more happiness, but don't know how to go about achieving this happiness.

In more than 25 years of working with people in business, education, marriage and family settings, I have come in contact with individuals who have achieved great levels of success, but have found themselves spiraling downward after their goals are met. Their desire for creating healthy growing relationships with the people they love soon left. Their personal, public and spiritual expectations were at an all-time low and they were not moving forward.

Creating Your Own Map

To create higher levels of personal success you need a map. Moving in the Right Direction is that map. This map includes simple and practical strategies that are based on an easy-to-use plan – one that guides people toward their own ideas of continuous success. Most people encounter problems while striving for success and it affects them in numerous ways and I suspect some of these problems may be familiar to you.

Change Your Thinking

These are deep problems, painful problems that quick fixes won't solve. You can choose the easy way out and not deal with your problems, but when you avoid your problems you allow them to grow into larger and more difficult problems.

I know that it's difficult to put your problems aside when you're feeling bad or your life is upside down. It's even more difficult when you love the people that you're having problems with..

If you want to change your situation, you have to first be willing to change your thinking. You must be willing to think it through and then take the proper action.

Family Pressures Can Take a Toll on You

As a child, my parents worked long hours to support our family and during my high school years I didn't see much of them. They didn't spend much time meeting new people or having fun. They never seem to have time for anything except us children and work. Some of my most painful memories are the times my parents argued and fought. Family pressures had taken a great toll on them so they decided to separate from one another.

After about a year of separation they filed for their divorce. Right about the time they were contemplating divorce I was dating a popular athlete that was in the eleventh grade. He was captain of three sports: football, basketball and track. The stress of my family falling apart caused me to turn to him for the answers to all my problems.

It was as if I turned my whole life over to him, and thus, he began to raise me in the place of my parents. He gave me love, attention and nurturing at the moments I needed it most. For two years he became the only person I shared my family crisis with and before I realized it I was so emotionally involved with him that I became pregnant. This made things worst.

Scared, Ashamed and No Place to Go

So, there I was a scared sixteen year old girl, pregnant, feeling abandoned and who could have ended up like so many other girls in my shoes: single, on welfare, uneducated, and struggling to make a living with next to nothing. But I wasn't going to settle for that. On the day I found out that I was pregnant I decided to continue with my plan to move forward. I yearned to succeed.

I was so ashamed of becoming pregnant that I did everything possible to hide it from the world. I even came close to dropping out of school. It was a very difficult time for me because not only were my friends ridiculing me, my parent's friends were discussing me in negative ways in my presence. They talked about me as if I wasn't there. I listened as my heart filled with pain. I felt like a failure. I didn't know what to do and many times I contemplated giving up just to make the pain go away. But guess what I persevered and fought to move forward. Thank God I did.

Ending a Relationship Is Sometimes Best

Then one day I heard my mother talking on the telephone to one of her friends, telling them how she was going to force me to marry the baby's father. I was terrified at the thought of marrying someone I didn't think that I loved enough to marry. I knew that this would move me in the wrong direction.

He was leaving for college, my parents were divorced and I was feeling abandoned. I called him and decided I would beg him not to go, but when I began to talk to him I couldn't manage to get the words out. I just couldn't see myself begging. My pride wouldn't let me. I didn't want to be a thorn in his side, nor a crutch. I wanted to go to college too.

The next day my boyfriend came over and told me that he wanted to talk to me before he went to college. I thought he was going to tell me he had changed his mind about leaving me and our unborn child. I was hopeful that he would stay and go to a college at home, but as he spoke to me his voice trembled and he lowered his head. I knew then that something was terribly wrong with what he was about to say.

He informed me that he was still going to college and he had another girlfriend and she was also pregnant. I was devastated, and full of so many mixed emotions. As he talked I cried. I was so out done that I yelled out to him, "What about me?" "What about our baby?" "What about my life, our future, our relationship, my education?" How could I possibly finish school now, I wondered? But just as quickly as I yelled out to him, I also restrained myself.

I looked into his eyes, calmed myself down and told him, "If I have to die trying I will graduate from high school and college. I was angry; I was upset; I was literally mad. So on that terrible day I decided to never ask him for help raising my child. I asked him to leave in the calmest voice that I could muster up. I struggled to find the words to tell him that I never wanted to see him again. He kept trying to explain and apologize, but I was in so much pain I couldn't stand to hear his voice, so I screamed for him to leave.

All connections to him ended for me that day. I knew there was no turning back. There was no way I could take him back, but now - what was I to do? There was no time for a pity party.

No Time for a Pity Party

There were no excuses to be made and no time for a pity party. The only thing that any girl in this kind of predicament can do is become as self-sufficient as possible. She has to pull herself together and map out a plan that can increase her chances of succeeding. Only then can she really move forward.

In my case, I had to move forward so that I could take care of my child. Off and on I would ask myself. "What am I to do?" I was terrified. I was only sixteen! How could I have made such a mess of my life? Even then I knew that I could not give up?

I kept saying to myself, "How can I turn this mess into something positive?" "How can I get past this moment of crisis? I had to remain determined in the face of defeat?" *"There was no time for a pity party!"* So, I made up my mind that I wasn't going to give up. This is definitely the kind of attitude you should have when life seems to be taking you backwards. I thought deeply. Then I concluded that I would not give in, give up or give out.

Refuse to Give Up, Give In or Give Out

Have you ever gone through moments when you wanted to give up, give in or give out? Have you ever been confused, scared and unsure? Maybe your situation was worse than some and not quite as bad as others. Either way throughout your ups and downs you'll have to reach deep inside and find the strength that you need to take the proper action.

Instead of giving up, I want you to find the reasons to hold on and persevere. Instead of giving in I want you to find ways to take responsibility for your mistakes. Instead of giving out I want you to reach deep down inside of yourself and find the strength to do what is necessary to help yourself. That's what I want you to do from this day forward.

I am not any stronger or smarter than you. My only strength is my will power to get through tough times. I refused to give up, give in or give out and that has made all the difference in the world.

Make and Keep Promises to Yourself

I want you to know that even though things will sometimes look hopeless, and you might be going through tough times it's important for you to change any negative directions your life is going. You must not wait on anyone else to do it for you. You can't harp on the guilt you feel for making a life mistake and you cannot feel sorry for yourself.

Promise yourself that you will have no pity parties. Promise yourself that you will continue to work each day to improve your life. Promise yourself that when you have to, you will take small steps that will help move you in a direction that will improve your standards of life. You have to begin immediately – follow your own path to extraordinary success.

Success Begins With Successful Thoughts

No matter how bad things are, and no matter what may happen there are effective ways to pick yourself up, brush off, and change things for the better. You must never give in, give up or give out.

By putting your own strategies in place so that you can succeed you learn that success begins with successful thoughts. To become successful you have to make commitments to reach our goals.

It's Not the Experience, It's the Procedure

All too often, we think our goals are all about the result. We see success as an experience that can be achieved and completed. Here are some common examples…

- Many people see health as an experience: *"If I just lose 20 pounds, then I'll be in shape."*
- Many people see entrepreneurship as an experience: *"If we could get our business featured in the New York Times, then we'd be set."*
- Many people see art as an experience: *"If I could just get my work featured in a bigger gallery, then I'd have the credibility I need."*

Those are just a few of the many ways that we categorize success as a single event. But if you look at the people who are consistently achieving their goals, you start to realize that it's not the experience or the results that make them different. It's their commitment to the procedure. They fall in love with the daily practice, not the individual experience.

What's funny, of course, is that this focus on the procedure is what will allow you to enjoy the results anyway. If you want to be a great writer, then having a best-selling book is wonderful. But the only way to reach that experience is to fall in love with the procedure of writing.

If you want the world to know about your business, then it would be great to be featured in S*uccess M*agazine. But the only way to reach that experience is to fall in love with the procedure of marketing.

If you want to be in the best shape of your life, then losing 20 pounds might be necessary. But the only way to reach that experience is to fall in love with the procedure of eating healthy and exercising consistently.

If you want to become significantly better at anything, you have to fall in love with the procedure of doing it. You have to fall in love with building the identity of someone who does the work, rather than merely dreaming about the experience that you want.

Commit to having a never give up attitude. To help you when times are difficult and you don't know what to do … here are small steps that will move you toward your success.

We have to work daily to become the person you want to be. Because we expect to improve our conditions, we have unconscious patterns that express our effectiveness, or ineffectiveness. We refer to these patterns as our good or bad expectations. Our expectations are very similar to our mindsets. We weave strands of our personal, public and spiritual expectations into our lives every day until they are a natural part of our success process.

Apply Effort, Energy and Commitment

Just because we want more out of life doesn't mean we will automatically get more from life. It isn't that simple. We have to utilize our opportunities. We have to apply effort, energy, commitment, and become dedicated if we want to improve our lives. Quite simply: if we are going to achieve our desired goals we have to work for our success every day.

Our hardships, bad times and negatives in life have an abundant pull on us, more than we ever believe or understand. Having a healthier, happier and more resilient mindset involves getting rid of those things that violate human effectiveness. It means getting past those things that wounded us in the first place. When we experience things like anger, procrastination, impatience, frustration, criticalness, and selfishness it means we need to do something that will assist us in making changes in our lives.

Achieving success takes a great amount of effort and as we strive to achieve our personal and professional goals we have to work toward consistent improvement. Getting past our negative thoughts, feelings and experiences will help us move toward our desired successes.

May the Force Be With You?

Now that you've worked hard try to bring forth the force to pull things together. Let's examine your force a little deeper. The force that pulls us toward our goals is our directional map, which also helps us get where we want to be in life. It is with this same force that we keep our world together and our lives in order.

This force is such a powerful force that if we use it effectively we can create and establish continued happiness and success in our lives. This force is our inner power and dedication to get things done. This is the same force that keeps us from giving in, giving up or giving out. It is a very powerful part of us. This force is a power to be reckoned with.

Create a Personal to Do List

In the course of continuing to be the person you want to be - consider the following 10-Step Process. Do this daily, but do not treat it as a chore. You will need a writing pad, pen or pencil.

1. Construct a short-term to-do-list.

Make a list of those things that you need to do immediately, so that you can reduce any unnecessary small problems. List every small task that you have been blocking out or refusing to get done. Each day work on your list by doing it and then scratch off completed tasks on the list as you complete them. Seeing the list shorten as you complete tasks will help you internalize success. Work on all tasks from this list. Don't give up. It reduces stress and frees your mind for more focus.

2. Create a long-term list of things to do.

Organize another list of all the long-term things you need to do in order to keep moving forward. This helps you focus on projects that need to be completed so you can get closer to your final goals. It gives you a record of your day-to-day accomplishments and achievements.

Long term accomplishments help you achieve goals and interrupt any thoughts of self-pity. It's constructive busyness.

3. Make phone calls and schedule new appointments.

Schedule appointments and meetings with people that you feel can help you get closer to your goals. Align the people that you need for each project. Make appointments with offices and programs that will help you. There are many programs that provide helpful information and aide.

4. Apply or order info from programs that will help you.

Become acquainted with the services and programs that help you achieve small goals and reach your bigger goals. Complete all necessary paperwork and be sure to turn it in before any deadlines or cut off dates.

5. Improve your education and/or get training.

Improving your educational standing will enhance and improve who you are. Gaining more knowledge will add more sparks to your conversation and your life.

6. Treat yourself good daily.

Watch how much you eat and monitor what you eat. Get plenty of sleep; exercise daily; take medications correctly; and avoid stress. Be good to yourself every day.

8. Continue to learn everything you can.

Learn as much as you can about careers, professional memberships, colleges and advancement programs. It gives you better opportunities to receive promotions, job advancements or career improvements.

9. Do positive things that keep you from sulking and feeling sorry for yourself.

   Keep busy and talk to people who have positive impacts on your life. Keep a positive journal so you can record the good things that happened to you and for you.

10. Develop a connection to a higher source of power.

    Read inspirational books, pray and meditate daily. Having a spiritual connection with a higher source will enable you to get through difficult times. This higher connection will give you the strength to move forward on a continuous basis.

A Moving Thought

Letting go doesn't mean giving up, but rather accepting that there are things that you must change.

Chapter 4

Mindset 3

Keep Moving Forward

This chapter will help you design a plan to change your life.

The New You

You have to keep moving if you want to get somewhere in life. So, here you are, ready to begin changing your life. You're ready to move in a different direction than what you've been going. You only need to look to your natural self to see that change is a natural part of the life-cycle. If you have a feeling that you want to change the direction you are going, listen to it. Recognize this as a call from your highest self that you are ready for transformation and renewed personal growth.

If you have seen two or more of these signs, it's a good indication that it is time to start making some alterations to your life, your career, your goals and your future. As you continue to uncover how to maximize your gift and find the best opportunity to use your talents.

Here are 12 practical goals for your future that will help you smoothly transition when you are contemplating making positive changes.

1. Take Up An Idea

It all starts with a great idea! Have you come up with a concept for a small business? Have you been secretly wanting to advance up the chain of command at work, but can't find the right course that might get you there? Can you potentially see a better way of doing things in your everyday life?

One of the biggest signs that you are ready to move forward in your life is that you feel inspired by a persistent idea. According to a celebrated Indian philosopher, Vivekananda, you should "take up one idea. Think of it, dream of it, and live on that idea. Let the brain, muscles, nerves, every part of your body, be full of that idea. This is the way to success."

Your idea does not have to be groundbreaking; it could even be something quite simple, such as finding a few extra hours a week to devote to your passion.

2. Identify Your Goals

Another sign that it's time to stop thinking and start doing is that you have clearly identified your goals. We all have different goals and our goals shift and change throughout our lives as our priorities move.

What's missing? Do you have a personal interest you'd like to pursue? Are you looking to start a new career? Are you hoping to gain more skills? Do you want to start a small business? If you know what you want to achieve, no matter what it is, then half the battle is already won. Get some advice, research online, or choose a short course to introduce yourself to a network of people who might be able to inspire you and help you. If you have already identified your goals, then this is a sure sign that you are ready to move forward.

3. Make Some Time

Just about every adult claims to be "time poor". We all have amounts free time available to us, and we just need to make our free time goals a priority.

Fitness guru and self-proclaimed nerd, Steve Kamb has said, "Your priorities, whether you say so or not, are where you choose to spend those hours. Make the most of them! It's amazing how much time you can find when you minimize the things that aren't important to make room for the things that are." If you find that you have some extra time in your schedule for whatever reason, this could be another great indication that it's time to make some a move in your life.

4. Allow Something New to Happen

Boredom is one of those messages from your intuition that a new move is needed. It's a signal that your energy is being drained and that something new and positive needs to happen.

Are you bored with your current situation? I suggests that you should, "bear in mind that the change that's required may simply be a shift in attitude or a new way of approaching something. It could also mean it's time to take action and make an outer, tangible move in your life."

We all get bored from time to time with our day to day activities and tasks, it's when this shifts from being a slight annoyance to a persistent feeling of boredom that we should take heed and start to move some things in our lives around.

5. Have a Plan

It doesn't need to be perfect or set in stone. All you need is the very next step! Not all of us are great planners. In fact, some people are so lousy at planning that they drift through life and never achieve any of the goals that they hope for.

Usually these people lack focus and a plan. They are 'dreamers' who fail to see the next step on their journey. Any goal looks huge when viewed from the end point. It's only when we break up a goal into smaller chunks that we get somewhere. If you have a plan, even if it's only a vague plan, that's a great indication that now, is the time to make a positive change in your life. Remember, you need to have a clear end goal. Change brings growth and growth allows you to release the past and gives you an opportunity to do something new and different.

6. Detox the Bad and Let the Good Come In

Having the feeling that you 'want to do a detox' is like waving a red flag to the Universe shouting at the top of your lungs, "I am ready for better things." Detoxing helps you avoid or get rid of a few bad habits. Doing a detox allows flow to happen inside your body and in your life. If you are feeling like now is the time to do a detox, listen to this urge and stay alert for possibilities to unfold.

7. Quit an Addiction

Wanting to stop eating foods that are bad for you is a classic sign that you are ready for something bigger to open up in your life. In my early 20's, I enjoyed being an eater of too many starchy foods, but with each year that passed I developed an uncomfortable relationship with starch. One taste of it mysteriously turned into more. Over the years, I became aware that starch was not serving me any good. I secretly desired to stop but I didn't know how. Fast-forward to today, I can tell you that giving up eating starches was one of the best decisions I have ever made. When you give up an addictive habit you get rewarded many times over. If something within you is ready to quit an addiction, really listen to it. Find support, educate yourself and surround yourself with people who have done what you want to do.

8. Lose Unwanted Weight

Having personally lost over 50 pounds and worked with many women wanting to 'lose weight," I discovered that this desire has little to do with losing weight and more to do with cultivating self-love. My experience has shown me that permanent weight loss happens when we choose to start healing our lives. To lose weight for good, the first thing to do is to stop dieting and start healing from within. When we create a healthy relationship with our body, and ourselves, weight loss can happen naturally and easily.

9. Pay-Off Debt

Having big amounts of debt is a sure-fire way to feel trapped and stuck. Debt can make you feel heavy and frustrated. If you have the feeling that you want to 'get on top of your money situation' by paying off debts, take action immediately!

Take responsibility for your finances. With small, baby steps you give yourself the chance to create a feeling of internal freedom. This will leave you feeling empowered and strong, with the belief and knowledge that you can do what you want to do. Taking action to pay off debts will ripple out and positively affect other areas of your life.

10. Transition Your Life

When you want to end a relationship, it takes courage to listen. Let this be a powerful transition and use it as an opportunity for personal growth and transformation.

When a relationship ends, it inevitably brings change. If you are someone who is afraid of change, this may also bring on fear. Acknowledge your fears, but keep connecting to the power of courage as you focus on new possibilities. Trust your gut feeling and instincts. Ensure that you surround yourself with like-minded, supportive people in order to become happy and healthy from within.

11. Change Your Occupation

If you are feeling bored or just 'hate your job' this is a strong signal that you need to pay attention. You don't have to do anything radical or rushed. Just start by taking small steps. Ask yourself, "What do I love?" Experiment with doing different types of work. The Myers-Briggs test is a fast and easy way to find out what type of work might suit you.

12. Take Time to Travel

If you are experiencing 'itchy feet' and you want to pack everything in and go travelling, take the time to listen to this urge. If you are feeling a desire to get away, simply sit down and quietly ask yourself, 'What is this feeling about?' Even if you don't have a lot of money, realize that there are many creative ways that you can fund your dreams for adventure.

When you see improvement on the horizon, stay flexible in your approach to life. Allow yourself to see new possibilities as they emerge in the moment. Draw on the quality of courage to help you deal with the new. When you listen and act on the wisdom of your inner guidance, change will be the 'magic bullet' that will enable you to live a life that you love.

A Moving Thought

Open your eyes; look within.
Are you satisfied with the life you're living?
- Bob Marley

Chapter 5

Mindset 4: Taking Your Journey

In this chapter you will understand why taking your journey can assist in your personal and professional success.

Move Toward Your Highest Potential

M**ost of us look at the world** or around us and are made keenly aware of the need for change. We can ignore the crime, economics, deprivation, school conflicts, social ills, health challenges, hopelessness, homeless and poverty. Sometimes the need is so great that we get overwhelmed and retreat, seeing ourselves as powerless, like little pebbles in a pile of big rocks, with little or no ability to make a difference. I really do understand.

Oftentimes in as little as an hour, I'm forced to recognize many hard truths. I wake up and turn on my computer and as soon as I hit the internet logo, the first thing I'm faced with is bad news, bad relationships and bad karma. I often see teenagers or grown men handcuffed and carted off in patty wagons by police adding to the already overcrowded jail system. As I get dressed and head to perform my daily duties, I find myself dodging near accidents on cluttered highways and congested traffic on city streets.

It's only 8:00 AM and I want to turn around and go back home, where there's peace and quiet. I want to get back and bed and wake up again to a better day.

Instead I remain stuck in traffic and remind myself that Vanessa Williams, Oprah Winfrey, and Rosa Parks didn't make powerful changes in one day nor did they do it by turning back around. I think to myself how I can make a subtle change in my life and the lives of those around me. Maybe I could say some kind word or write some helpful words in one of my books that that would help someone else meet their challenges head on. Maybe I could teach someone a powerful lesson that might help them feel good and help them be more thankful for the life they are living.

When I decided to write my next book my mission was far bigger than simply putting words on paper. I wanted to provide a roadmap that women could be treated as special as a king or queen. I wanted women to read my books and feel like they were going on a restorative retreat where they could come and recharge themselves to go back out into the world and do the critical work that we all must do. The comments and reflections after reading my books that people have sent me is proof that my mission is being actualized and that's motivation for me to keep on keeping on. Consider these comments that were sent to me:

"I bought your book when I was at odds with myself, desperately needing clarity to reconnect and reacquaint myself with the person I am. After reading your book I am feeling stronger as an individual and now I feel that I can move forward and complete the tasks."

"I am reading this book with one purpose in mind, to become the best person that I be. I am now moving a direction that feels great and I have been renewed."

"All I needed was direction and a sense of order in my own life. Your book has helped me find my way."

Women from all over the world who have not read any of my books have been positively affected by other people who have spoken kindly about my lessons. You see how we are all diamonds in the rough?

We Are the Diamonds and Pearls of Life

While we shouldn't depend on others outside of ourselves to validate us, I have noticed a difference in the way we feel and treat each other once we gain knowledge. For so long because of broken spirits and our failure to recognize that we are the diamonds and pearls of life we think less of ourselves. We each have value, but most importantly we should not forget that the people in our lives have value too.

We are each architects of our own lives and women feel better about themselves when they are given positive strokes. They experience wonderful psychological and spiritual transformations. Deep inner shift in your reality occurs, aligning you with the creative energy of the universe.

Pick up the needle with me and make the first stitch on the canvas of your life. Open up the eyes of your inner awareness. Be still and wait expectantly. Knowing that the deviation of your daily life as it exists today are the golden threads of a potential abundance tomorrow.

Most of us live our lives at only a fraction of our potential. We tend to peek just beyond the surface of what is possible, failing to look any further. Maybe looking further is a challenge because most times we are afraid to commit, whether it's positive or negative. When our dreams stretch far beyond our comfort zone our subconscious often interrupts us with dream-shattering questions or statements that our loved ones make like these:

"You want to do what? How could you be so crazy to think that you could do that? "You love it because of what?" "It will never work." "A career like that takes a lot of sacrifices. You might as well give up on that thought."

Have you ever found yourself struggling with why people said or did something to discourage you? Did they do or say things that make you feel like a failure before you got started on your success journey? Did it make you struggle with self-doubt, anger, or resentment? Most of us have felt this way at one time or another.

As the dream shattering questions and statements continued did you want to quit? There are probably times in your life that you became doubtful and tuned out any possibility of succeeding. Don't feel bad about it because that's part of the process when you decide to take the success journey.

As an educator I've had the opportunity to meet thousands of people who have been in self-doubting situations. Three things are significantly important about people who doubt themselves.
They feel that …

1. …life is empty and they aren't living the life they were born to live.

2. …life is incomplete when they are not participating in their divinely appointed purpose.
3. …success is distant when specific steps in the right direction are not taken.

I've been in this doubtful and distant place too, but I want you to remember one thing …. And that is you've got to go through the ups and downs of the journey to get through the journey. It's all a part of the process. It's all a part of shaping your life and preparing for success. If you don't give up the rewards are fantastic!

Get Your Life in Shape

When our lives are out of shape and we need to get fit or rid of excess baggage we would probably hire a professional of some kind who could help us get it all together. Wouldn't it be great if we could do this for all parts of our life? Shape our lives and overcome many unforeseen obstacles that get in the way of us living the life we love. This would at least make us feel better about how we are living.

It's simple; if you think you can achieve your goals and you believe that there's a way to achieve these goals, you tend to work toward those goals with a higher level of confidence. So it's safe to say that when we see our life getting to a place of happiness and we see things finally coming together we tend to feel better about the shape we are in, thus feeling good about the shape our lives are in too.

Let's look at it this way: When our bodies are in shape we feel good about ourselves; our self-esteem is high and we strut instead of walk. When our lives are in shape we feel more successful and our ability to meet our problems head-on are done with confidence and assuredness. We trust our decision making and are less doubtful and uncertain.

Radical Changes through Deliberate Actions

Your strong belief in yourself will guide you into the abundance that life has to offer. In the process of moving in the right direction I want you to stretch yourself by making radical changes through small, deliberate actions. Whenever the time comes that you are at the end of your life, God doesn't want you to look back and regret *"the something more"* that was out there, and you never got it. Or that you spent too much time focused on money, things, or outward appearances and not enough time working on you or creating experiences with the people you love.

The seams of your life are bursting with possibilities and you should unleash them so you can live at your highest potential. Your highest potential is not to be confused with your highest performance level. I am not talking about adding more activities to your already busy schedule. I'm talking about living a fuller, richer life with maximum effort, more fun, and tremendous benefits.

Serve the World with Your Natural Gifts

Your life should empower you to serve the world with your natural gifts and talents, while being compensated for doing so. Trusting your inner voice nurtures you with a cushion of abundance in every area of your life so that you have the freedom to make choices that reflect your innermost desires.

As you take your own success journey you will experience principles that points you onto your path of extraordinary success – a path that helps you stay on course. This journey is filled with all sorts of positive strategies.

This journey toward success is focused on the "whole you" and true success - magnificent success - the kind that truly expresses who you are. This includes your…

- Spiritual life
- Physical health and environments
- Relationships
- Work
- Finances and resources

So often our role models are stereotypes of what success should be; they represent only the career or financial picture of a person. Did you know that you can have financial success and still not have a successful life? If you choose to buy into stereotypes that overemphasize career and money and de-emphasize health, fulfillment, relationships and intimacy you will find yourself pursuing a weak substitute for true success - and you'll be deeply disappointed and dissatisfied.

Define Your Own Success

Success is unique for each of us, but we must define it for ourselves. Without a definition for success how will you know when or if you are successful? The answer is simple: You won't. However if you fail to define success, the world will define it for you - and the world's definition may lead you to a cycle of failure, emptiness, or living below your life's potential - none of which is true to your divinely ordained path.

A few years ago, I helped people write their own books. One of the most important lessons I acquired was to help my clients define success before we proceeded with a client. Otherwise we would find ourselves in the middle of a project, doing the things that would lead to success as we define it, but not necessarily as the client defined it. Sometimes our definition would far exceed the clients. At other times the client's expectations might exceed our capabilities.

For our clients to succeed and for our services to be of the most value we needed a clear understanding of what they were looking for. Not only did this understanding help us reach the desired goals, it also helped us recognize early on whether a client's definition of success was too big, too narrow or too small.

Plan What Successes You Want

Clearly defining what you want and by what date you want it is the main ingredient of success. Once you are specific about who, what, when and how - your wheels start turning and you can get busy planning what successes you want.

When you have a target to aim at and begin to move in the direction that you're aiming for - a life of success is much greater than if you didn't have a target.

I suggest employing the power of the written word as you create your own unique definition of success. Begin thinking of ways in which your views of success have been shaped - possibly even skewed - by other people in your life or by society as a whole.

Keep a Private Journal or Notebook

I had been laid off work. This was the first time in my life since I began to work that I had ever been off work for more than 6 days. To help me deal with my discomfort and developing depression I started journaling. I recorded everything that was important in my life. Every time I felt bad I wrote it down. Every time I wanted to cry I wrote it down. I wrote why I was feeling the way I felt. Believe me my positive journal helped me get through my most difficult times. Tweet me @emp55 on how you have reached some of your most wanted goals.

Consider these 8 ways that keeping a journal can help you reach your goals and track your feelings:

1. Keeping a journal requires us to write out our goals.

2. Writing out our goals or feelings provides the opportunity to articulate them clearly and makes their achievement appear closer.

3. A journal serves as a permanent record of feelings or personal progress. Success can be quickly forgotten. And when it is, it becomes easy to get frustrated. As with any pursuit, there are times we may feel like we have not accomplished anything despite all the invested

effort and energy. During those moments, it is helpful to look back and be reminded of past successes.

4. Writing requires us to think through the whys and the how's. When we sit down behind a blank computer screen or sheet of paper and begin to write out what we accomplished during the day, we are forced to think through our process on a deeper level. The discipline forces us to answer the difficult questions of "why," "how," or "why not?" The answers to these questions are helpful as we move forward to repeat successes and avoid mistakes; they can also be therapeutic.

5. A journal proves we have solved problems in the past. Whether we are chasing a physical goal (run 26.2 miles), a career goal (start my own business), or a personal goal (become a better father), not every step in our pursuit is going to be easy… goals worth pursuing never are. At some point, we are required to overcome adversity. The next time we face it, we'll find motivation and strength in our written record of overcoming it in the past.

6. Keeping a journal naturally reminds us to articulate next steps. It is difficult to look back without also looking forward. As a result, when we journal, we naturally

begin to look forward. And the next step becomes easier to see, visualize and expect.

7. Writing reminds us to think beyond the obvious. Always looking for "material to journal" has caused me to understand the value of simplicity and minimalism in areas I would not normally have seen it — whether it be an article in the newspaper, an advertisement on television, or a conversation with a friend. Likewise, writing causes us to become more intentional in any pursuit — and to find inspiration beyond the obvious places right in front of us.

8. Even a private journal provides accountability. As we script our journey, we find accountability — not to the written word, but to ourselves. Our past success and perseverance compels us forward. We can see how far we've come, how much we have left to accomplish, and why giving up would be foolish.

9. A written account allows our story to inspire others. Our journal is our story. It is our account of moving from Point A to Point B. And when we share it, it can inspire others to do the same.

A Moving Thought

Remember your true wealth can be measured,
Not by what you have, but by who you are.

Chapter 6

Mindset 5: Increasing Your Power

In this chapter we will learn how to take on new adventures instead of them taking you on.

Establish Your Own Path

In the late seventies, inventor Art Fry was frustrated because the notes he had wrote for his hymnal kept falling out on the floor. His most disturbing problem was not new to most people, but on this particular day he came up with a solution for this problem. Fry was employed in the retail tape division of 3M and along with others he had been trying to come with an idea that would put to use a low track adhesive that another employee, Dr. Spencer Silver had invented. Even though Fry's idea was simple, it was creative enough for most of us to ask ourselves,

"Why didn't I create this?" Today his idea is now a multimillion dollar creation that we know as 'Post it notes. It can be found in every office and many homes in America.'

Our most creative ideas are born out of a need to find an answer to a problem. We are all capable of being creative in our way for whatever reason our creativity is sparked, but the creative juices I'm speaking of are those that can help serve you daily to spark your life goals.

Creativity Sparks Creativity

When I speak of creativity I speak of the creativity a person that will keep the love alive in their marriage, the creativity needed to teach a child who has learning disabilities, the creativity needed to help someone who is suffering and you finding a way to help ease the pain or stop the pain.

Fluctuating your energy to a broad scope of creativity, helps you begin to see your creative talents – and raise the value of them. Creativity is the ability to bring to life something of purpose, value and appeal that did not previously exist. Apply the principle of creativity to all areas of your life; from artistic endeavors to business objectives, from our relationships to our spiritual lives. We create when we are creative. Whether you are creating a business, a song, a job, a caring relationship, a healthier mindset, a healthier body, a book, a new look, career or cure, selecting to be creative will release previously underdeveloped ideas and abilities.

Despite the fact that the world may applaud you for such efforts determine if these goals authentically connected to you or are they meaningless and unimportant in your goal setting agenda?

Establish Your Personal Power

Establishing personal power is important when you stop spending precious time and energy pursuing goals that hold no true excitement for you. It's easy to follow the status quo and aim for personal access when your creative markers are out. Some of the most fruitful and satisfying paths are often the most creative. Those who found ways to think and act creatively usually find a great level of success. Creative ideas revolutionize entire industries, transform lives and influence our values.

With the achievement of every unauthentic goal, you will feel miscellaneous goals carrying you away from your ultimate fulfillment. We only need to look to companies that have successfully introduced new, over-the-top concepts to see that it's possible to build something from nothing.

We are often discouraged from pursuing things that are new and different because we are afraid that our ideas may fail. If you follow cultural expectations blindly and pursue wealth, power, or fame because you think that is what you are supposed to do, grabbing the brass rings will feel meaningless. If you lack the connection to your own values, then you may wake up one day having achieved your secondary goals, but feeling disconnected from your primary goals and ultimately feeling like a failure.

What Do You Really Desire

If you desire the corner office, but do not truly aspire to be there, the views of having this office won't leave you breathlessly happy. If success for you means living in the house on the hill and living a life of peaceful solitude, then you're going to have to find ways to move in the direction that brings those dreams and wishes to your life. Tweet me your single most important dream @emp55.

If you desire a fortune like Oprah Winfrey or Bill Gates and only want to privately measure your prosperity, the money in the bank will never meet your deepest desires. Acquiring a dream that is really not your dream can be enticing, but it will never really satisfy your true needs. You will still feel empty in the end. Your dreams should be your dreams, not the dreams that someone else has dreamed for you. The point I'm making is… it should be your chosen path to take in order to get to your dream life, so naturally you must choose what is really going to satisfy you. It must be your life's dream.

What Does Personal Power Really Mean

Having personal power not only prepares you to become a new and better person, it helps you maintain a level of fortitude. When you are trying to move toward your highest potential it's not easy. When you are at your highest level in life you are usually more willing to try new things and you probably feel like you're taking on new adventures instead of them taking you on.

When you're at your lowest level it's difficult to take on something new. Most times when you are at your lowest you feel drained, pressured, out of sync and less capable. So, like most people who find themselves in a challenging position, its easy to give up and not try any more.

You can stay in your rut or you can start doing things that will help you get out of a rut. Here's how:

- Determine what personal power means to you.
- Determine what cultural falsehoods are holding you back.
- Examine them, then determine if any of these negative thoughts really ring true for you.

Does importance, clout, VIP status, luxury cars, affluent addresses, a high society marriage and expensive watches hold true when you think of success? These are only external measurements of what our society generally views as symbols of success. Perhaps it's because these are markers that are the most universally appealing.

If these success elements are calling your name, you can weave your vision of success into them. You can pursue your dreams and work toward earning the kinds of rewards that bring you joy. However many people pursue these popular trappings and/or goals without really knowing why. Perhaps they become entangled in the web of keeping up with other people's dreams.

The best thing we can do for ourselves to get out of our ruts is stop measuring our happiness and our successes by other people's ideas of success. We can stop measuring our happiness by what our family or friends decide our happiness should be. We can create our own standards for what we feel is our true happiness.

We can decide that no matter how simple or grand our level of happiness or success is we will begin today by basing it on the dreams and goals that we feel the most passionate about. And along the way we have to remember - what makes other people happy or successful will not necessarily make us happy or successful. We have to find ways to measure our own success.

Measuring Your Own Success

When success is pursued as proof of your value, you are giving your life and efforts over to the assessment of others. On the other hand, when success is pursued as the position of your innermost values, and your goals become the validation of your inner truth, you are honoring your presence on earth as meaningful and authentic.

Observers who calculate and evaluate whether you have met a standard established by society can assess success externally; however, at the end of the day, when it's all said and done there is either a peaceful feeling within you or there is emptiness. The peaceful feeling signals that you have lived up to your own expectations and personal visions.

If you are experiencing emptiness it's a clue that you were striving toward a definition of success and fulfillment that was never yours to begin with. If you are feeling peacefulness you are probably on the right track to finding your success. Determine if you are feeling emptiness or peacefulness.

Envision Your Vision

To help you convey your vision, I give you the following exercise, which can help you visualize what will bring you fulfillment. Complete the following sentences by writing down your responses. Use this page, your journal or on a blank sheet of paper. It is not sufficient merely to complete the sentences in your mind as you read them; you must commit your answers to paper.

You can change what you wrote after you see them in print, but make sure you write them down. Writing them down is the key to successful visualization efforts. Tweet me your number one vision @emp55.

1. The people I know are successful because…

   ____

   ____

2. I only feel successful when I am…

   ____

   ____

3. My ideas of success are…

   ____

   ____

4. I feel more successful when I am involved in …

   ____

   ____

5. If I were to die today and people had to talk about my success they would say…

   ____

   ____

For example, as a response to statement number two you might list the things you have already did that made you feel successful in life and continue to make you feel like a success. You might even list people you don't know personally, but who you admire from afar, such as an accomplished athlete, a celebrity or a respected talk show host. By identifying your role models, you can see whom you admire and then specify what attributes and behaviors they have that you choose to emulate.

Here's an example: Juanna listed her friend Tina as someone she admired for fulfilling her goals. Tina was an intelligent woman and although it was unheard of for a paralyzed woman to live a totally successful life she fought to live her life independently. Despite the strong objections of her family, the disapproval of her doctor and numerous physical obstacles placed in her path by this overwhelming disease Tina attended real estate school, went to income tax school and earned licenses in both.

Upon further reflection, Juanna saw that it was Tina's courage in the face of adversity that she was drawn to and realized that it was this quality she wanted to possess within herself. When Juanna found several lumps in her breast it was Tina's strength and determination she called upon. Juanna called upon her spiritual connection with Tina to help her find the inner strength to overcome this illness.

Another example is the fourth statement

"I feel more successful when I am involved in"...

Using the word 'I' gives you the chance to try and get involved in things that will make you really feel successful. It also helps with your future aspiration to see how you will feel. There is something very powerful about putting "I" in front of all your desires. Clearly stating "I will make you feel successful: When I am able to pay all of my bills" puts you into the vision of feeling successful. Putting "I" into the statements gives you ownership over your wishes. Don’t be afraid to use “I” when you are visualizing your dreams and goals.

Examining Your Life

When you start examining your life you must be painfully honest about what you want to accomplish. It can be a little uncomfortable writing down your dreams, hopes and desires. They become real because they have a tendency to sound ambitious, but unless you allow yourself to imagine your ideal life, you can never begin to make it happen.

Now, for a moment, imagine yourself at the end of your life. Looking back can be helpful when you're trying to articulate what it is you hope to accomplish during your lifetime. Let's try it.

Find a quiet and comfortable place you can focus without distractions. Begin by writing your very own life story as it reads up to this moment. Start anywhere you like in the story. Anywhere you decide to start is the beginning as you see it. Write it in past tense and in third person. For example she was born in …"and so on. Include all those moments that you feel are relevant to your life

- your accomplishments, events, experiences and relationships that have contributed to your development.

While you're writing don't judge or edit what you write. Rather put your wishes, hopes, dreams, goals, and aspirations down on paper as they come to your mind. Later you can edit what you wrote if you choose. After you are finished, look closely at what you did with your life and ask yourself if this is what you would like to become the reality. If it isn't, revise or rewrite it. When you are satisfied with it, put it in a place where you can reread it on a regular basis and begin to strategize how you will make these successes come true.

Your Success Has Its Own Thumbprint

The most defining description about moving in a success filled direction is that it can't be universally interpreted. Each person has his or her own vision of what it means to succeed and become more successful, which is every bit as personal and unique as a thumbprint. Every person moves toward success in his or her own way and in his or her own time. You are no different.

The secret to achieving your own success is to search your heart for what matters to you and set the standards of what direction you are headed and then decide what direction you would like to go. Your knowledge and chances of succeeding can multiply a thousand fold. Once you take the courageous leap and begin the journey toward personal fulfillment you can ultimately live the satisfying life you want and deserve.

Allow Time for New Beliefs to Set In

When you decide to make changes in your life, you might want to see these changes happen immediately. This is unrealistic, Remember, it took many years for you to get into your present mindset. It is unreasonable to demand total reversal on your bad mindsets and negative patterns by the next day. Allow reasonable time for your new beliefs to take hold, and then you can integrate them into the other beliefs you have.

Each day do something small a little bit different and soon you'll see yourself doing more and being more for yourself..

A Moving Thought

Sometimes taking baby steps are the next best thing to achieving your goals.

Chapter 7

Mindset 6: You Have What It Takes

In this chapter you will understand how having strength in your beliefs can help you get ahead.

You Can Make Things Happen

Before you can actively decide what you really want in life you have to believe that you can do the things you set out to do.

There is this thing we call low self-confidence that I believe to be a virus. It's an epidemic among people whose happiness level has been reduced. This virus is also the root cause of many other problems people encounter; from overeating to alcoholism. When you neither like nor respect yourself you might get involved with people who are either uncaring or unworthy. You might choose jobs that prove you are overqualified and underpaid. You might even make unfortunate choices and get involved with a partner who is mentally and physically abusive based on what you think you deserve.

There are simple ways that you can move more toward your desired dreams by imagining that you are climbing uphill. Your dream is there-uphill sitting on top of the hill. You have to climb up that hill in order to retrieve your dreams. Every step forward, every move you make toward your dream feels like an uphill battle. Even when you get tired you have to rest yet remain focused on the dream. Because you know you've come too far to stop now. You look up and finally realize that you are almost there, so you can't turn back now. You have to keep going, maybe a little slower than when you started but still you can't give up now. Once you finally reach the top you look around, catching your breath and taking a short rest, getting regrouped, refueling, relieved as you relish the glory of your accomplishment.

The truth is you know this is just the beginning of your true journey. You realize that you are moving forward, finally moving in the right direction. You are happy and satisfied. You are ready to push forward; on to the next goal because now you know that you can do it.

Wherever you are on that hill – the bottom, the middle, the side or maybe even at the top, you are not the only one. I've been there too, waiting and waiting then winning. As you have read I have fallen off the hill a few times, but I got back up, dusted myself off and started again.

I want you to see your uphill battle as a means to your end; a way to move forward, a way to reach your goals. Your goals are your climb to the top. Now ask yourself what hill are you willing to climb to reach your goals? Tweet me your answer @emp55

I want you to break down your climb into tiny pieces so that it won't be so overwhelming. You know yourself better than anyone so be honest with what keeps you motivated and moving forward. Here are twenty two habits that prove you have what it takes

1. Appreciate yourself.

It starts little-by-little each day. It encourages you to feel good about yourself. Being able to graciously accept big and small compliments helps you learn to believe in yourself. When you appreciate yourself you are more effective in both personal and professional life. Everyone has good points that they can call upon when they need them the most. To help strengthen your belief system start doing more things that you like to do.

2. Say and do positive things.

Starting today … there will be no more blaming the other person, no more self-pity and no thinking less of yourself.

Today you start doing positive uplifting things for yourself. Today you start concentrating on saying and doing things that will help you take the proper action. Read, study, listen to music, dance and do those things that make you feel good about yourself. This helps increase your internal encouragement. Saying and doing positive things allow you to put what you say into action.

3. Give yourself a break.

Don't take responsibility for things that you can't change or control. Let go of those things that bring your spirit down. Get rid of negative feelings by replacing them with feelings that are happier and more rewarding to your self-confidence. If you want to like yourself you'll have to be more loving and supportive of *yourself*.

4. Accept yourself.

Forgive yourself for those things that you did that weren't quite up to your expectations and then place all the good things that you've did in your memory so that you can call upon them when you need to feel better about yourself. Start today feeling good about the things you've done in your life. Congratulate yourself for those things that you like about yourself. Vow to change or correct those things you don't like about yourself.

5. Learn from your mistakes.

Try not to condemn yourself for your mistakes. We all make mistakes - it's normal and expected. Mistakes are usually not permanent; therefore, you can recover from most of them. Past personal experiences have a way of making us stronger if we recognize what we learned from the experience. No matter what mistakes you make, forgive yourself, and then work to improve your life by moving forward in a positive way.

6. Look your best at least 80% of the time.

It's difficult to look your best 100% every single day of your life, but looking your best 80% of the time will help you feel good on the inside and outside. Don't stress about looking too good, just keep yourself well-groomed and the rest will work itself out. No matter how you feel, put your best self out front. Looking your best helps boost your morale and gives you a positive outlook on life. It helps you feel good and others see a positive side of you.

7. Keep an empowerment photo album.

Keep photos of all the people you love, adore, and admire. It will help you feel good when you're feeling bad. If you find yourself feeling lonely or sorry for yourself and you need to feel cared for, take a look at your empowerment photo album to help you get through tough times. Seeing the people you love will lift your spirits. It's the best medicine for you during low times.

8. Stop blaming yourself.

By replacing blame with healthy thoughts you'll start feeling better about yourself and you'll soon start solving your problems. Replace your worries with positive actions and then use your positive energy to focus on solutions to your problems. Getting rid of the blaming attitude helps channel your energies in the right direction. Choose to stop blaming yourself and you'll have peace of mind.

9. Reprogram yourself.

Reprogramming your mind helps you better understand how to go about achieving what you want in life. Each time an event occurs in your life it stimulates an interpretation of that event in your mind. Even though you don't always hear your inner voice you can feel when it's trying to tell you something. You can always feel more than you can see. When you feel insecure all you have to do is work on reprogramming your mind to think better thoughts.

10. Keep a journal of things that are important to you.

Keeping a journal will remind you of the people and things you love the most. Be sure to include yourself. Make two lists; one list should include the things that make you happy and your second list will consist of those things that you desire most. As you record important moments you will become more in tune with what's important to you. Discover who you are and then enjoy your life more.

11. Take small steps to make positive changes.

When you take small steps you can steadily accomplish your goals without feeling overwhelmed or pressured. Small steps help your little victories feel like bigger accomplishments. Work to achieve victories as soon as you can - one step, one task, one day at a time.

12. Feel free to move forward.

As you work to accomplish your goals you'll probably remember those times that you didn't quite achieve them. Maybe you were waiting on someone else to tell you to do it, or maybe you weren't sure how to do it. Many times you wait on others to say its okay before you decide to make a move. You have to give yourself permission to take action.

13. Remain determined.

To get what you want you must build a strong foundation of determination. Focusing on the direction you want to go helps you remain determined to get there. With determination you consciously decide you are going to achieve your goals no matter what obstacles are in your way. Determination helps you realize and understand your hopes, ambitions and desires.

14. Be the best that you can be.

It's never too late to be the person you desire to be. As you take on challenges your confidence begins to rise and you start feeling better about yourself.

A large part of your uniqueness is expressed through the kind of work you chose. More education, professional training or hands-on experience might be needed to help you improve yourself. When you decide to be more of who you want to be it doesn't mean you have to let go of the things you believe in or release old mindsets, it simply means you're going to make changes in the way you think and feel. Positive decisions helps you become the best you can be.

15. Determine what your goals are.

Everyone has goals. They may be big or small, but still they are goals. To determine what your goals are you have to: (a) Have a plan of action. (b) Let go of those things that are holding you back (c) Make a list of your realistic goals. (d) Don't overwhelm yourself while trying to reach your goals. (e) Know what it is you don't want to do so you'll have time to discover what it is you would like to do. (f) Remain flexible so you'll be able make changes if your goals are unrealistic or unattainable.

16. Focus on what's really important.

Focus takes the roadblocks out of what you are trying to do. Making the important *"to do list"* helps you see what's most important. As you achieve your goals you can cross them off the list. When you see your goals being reached you can concentrate more on things that you feel are of greatest priority.

17. Find balance in your life.

In order to find the proper balance in life you have to figure out how to organize your life. If you direct all of your energy and attention to one thing – you lose sight of the world around you and as soon as something goes wrong with another part of your life you will fall apart. Balance enriches your life and gives your mind a chance to relax. It also helps you deal with life's disappointments. With balance; your mind can work on more than one thing at a time without feeling overwhelmed.

18. Tune in to what you say.

Words have power. What you say can stop you from achieving your goals. If you constantly tell yourself you *"can't"* you began to believe it. You have to change the things you say to yourself. Your subconscious mind tunes in to what you say. By altering the things that you say you can open many doors.

19. Listen to what you hear.

When you learn to pay attention to what other people say, you can better determine who the negative people are. People who give positive reinforcement increase your chances of success because they don't tamper with your self-esteem or positive mindset. Avoid listening to negative talk that strips you of the desire to reach goals.

20. Select your role models.

Role models are important when you are trying to create a better belief system. Role models should be smart, positive, nurturing, loving, sincere, and patient and should express levels of pride. Good role models bring out the best in you. When you create positive associations you bring positive influences.

21. Establish your ethical and moral code of conduct.

To establish your codes of conduct, your philosophy of life has to come from within. Perhaps the best codes of moral behavior can be summed up in one sentence: *'do unto others, as you would have them do unto you.'* It's important to understand your standard of personal conduct. To do this; know what is the lowest level you will not allow yourself to go.

22. Gain understanding.

You gain the most understanding when you take control of your life. Understanding will give you the power to look at things in such a way that you'll be able to cultivate your thoughts. Learn from those things that enable you to grow into a more insightful person. Understanding your purpose gives you advantages in life because it allows you to make better decisions about your life. When you understand who, what, and why of your life you are more liberated and powerful.

You *do* have what it takes. The controlling factor is in your personal discipline. Personal discipline is developed one act and one day at a time until it becomes a mindset. The challenge, then, is to succeed in each area of your life; which includes work, family, and business. After that, work smarter so that you can develop the wisdom to balance the ever-changing circumstances in your life.

A Moving Thought

"Years from now you will be disappointed by the things you didn't do than by the one's you did. Imagine, dream, explore, discover."

Chapter 8

Mindset 7: Making the Right Connections

In this chapter you will learn how to make connections and learn how to communicate from a personal level.

Connect with God, Yourself and Others

Consider for a moment the chain of events that led you to the life you are living right now. Isn't it amazing how one thing leads to another until we arrive at one particular moment and place in time? Sometimes it's the place we're supposed to be, and sometimes we simply know that another path awaits us as we continue to find it.

When it's not the correct path a persistent voice whispers softly but urgently. *"You're going in the wrong direction. There's a path over here with your name on it."* Even if we are unaware of where our path is, God will find a way to lead us to our destiny - and connect us with the right people. The universe seems to open at just the right moment that you need to connect. The key to your correct path is listening to what your life is trying to tell you. Follow the voice of your spirit and walk in your own unique direction. Don't be afraid. Fear is not the answer at this time. Here's a story that will help you understand my point.

Debra's Story

While enjoying a casual walk with a group of inspiring friends one Saturday, I asked Debra, how she got her start as a media communicator. Debra is a very energetic woman in her thirties, who had just resigned from her job with an upbeat radio show so that she could fully focus on her interior design business. It was a brave move, but Debra was up for the challenge. In less than two distinctive years she's gone from decorating and collecting furniture as a hobby to creating a line of distinctive furniture for upscale homes. Broyhill, Thomasville and other exclusive furniture stores across the world now carry her distinctive furniture collection.

Her journey began in April 2003 on an afternoon when she was taking a day from work to gather her thoughts. Debra turned on the television just in time to catch a daytime talk show host who was debating with the audience about relationships. Debra felt compelled to log on to the show's website and send an email expressing her thoughts about the subject. To her surprise she received a phone call from one of the producers from the show. They we're planning to tape another segment of the same show and wanted to consider Debra as a guest. She connected with the producer and had an upbeat conversation. While talking they briefly stumbled on Debra's favorite past time: designing furniture. It was a hobby born out of her childhood when she spent a lot of time bargain shopping with her grandmother. Creating a hand-drawn design and collecting odd shaped pieces of wood, glass and moldings was a passion that came naturally to her - and her love for wood and glass is very apparent to anyone who speaks to her.

The producer ended the conversation, saying "We'll get back in touch with you as soon as we decide when the show will be scheduled." Later that year when planning a show about people and their passions, the producer called and asked Debra to send some photos and maybe a sample of a small piece of furniture she had designed. The photos along with the samples she sent were an instant hit and they booked her for the show!

Inspired by the host who was none other than Oprah, words of encouragement flowed during the taping and Debra had an overwhelming response to her beautiful, yet oddly exquisite pieces.

Debra began taking the steps that led to the creation of her company, Debra's Eclectic Designs. She admits she wanted to, but would have never put her entrepreneurship into practice if things had not been placed so clearly in her path. She admits being featured on Oprah and hearing from retail stores around the country was a great boost to her ego. It was a series of connected events that pushed her in the right direction toward her unique path. She now uses her talents to help other people beautify their homes, not to mention the showrooms her collections appears in. And to think it all began on an afternoon she took off work, when she was watching television and listening to her intuition that said contact them. It was Debra’s inner voice prompting her to take action toward her dream. She was not afraid. It was that divine nudge from the universe that helped Debra move in a positive direction. - A direction that turned out to be just right for her.

Finding Your Own Path

Have you ever felt compelled to do something that seemed silly or inconsequential? Did it feel like some kind of divine nudge was taking place to encourage you to take a specific action? It happens that way sometimes. God uses divine moments to move us in a way that our path crosses at a specific moment.

The first step to finding your path is 'direction', the process that leads you toward finding what is designed especially for you. It may appear to some to be luck or chance, but it isn't. These compelling nudges happen to us every day and sometimes they happen many times throughout the day. These are divinely arranged directions we should take that spark action after listening to one's heart, mind and spirit.

Finding your direction is the core principle of this book. It is the leading foundation of your life's actions. It is also the invisible string that connects you with God, yourself and others. And it is the vital principle that helps you find your unique path to extraordinary success in life.

The second step to finding your direction is 'connection', the process of relating to a higher power, yourself and others. Connection helps you to find your path, stay on it, and then return to it when you stray. As you connect to your experiences, purposes, and possibilities you become more knowledgeable and sure about guiding your life in the right direction.

There are many directions you can go and many paths you can follow but only one is uniquely designed for you. It is the direction and path which life, though not always smooth is divinely arranged and perfectly connected to your experiences, talents, and authentic desires.

Connect, Disconnect and then Reconnect

As much as I hate to admit it, in my own life I have stood on that fine line where earth and heaven meet. My life-changing experiences of failure, confusion, frustration, defeat and feeling a lack of purpose had beaten me down.

My setbacks can be traced to connections that were disconnected. This disconnection came from my own desires and needs, my relationships, or other people whose presence and wisdom was unimportant to my well-being. At those times of frustration in my life, I found myself disconnecting with those people who mattered the most and would be able to help pull me through.

Nearly five years after I wrote my first book, I was financially stable but I felt as though my life was lacking professional and spiritual growth. At first, I didn't feel that I needed to pray as often, after all; things were going good for me. I was so busy living my own dream that I took little time for my family and friends and church. I found myself dreading the work I was once passionate about. You see, I was a schoolteacher in an inner city school and coached several sports. I enjoyed working with the girls whom I coached and I loved teaching school, but I wanted more. What I once loved with enthusiasm had become what I loved the least.

After about ten years of teaching I began to feel unfulfilled so I started working on my first book, something I had always dreamed of doing. I completed it in 9 months, promoted it from the trunk of my car and gained immediate attention from broadcast and print media. The book became a national best seller and I became a nationally known author. I was successful? I enjoyed meeting new people, appearing on the television and radio shows, but something that I longed for was still missing. I simply wasn't excited about my work. Why was I feeling guilty about my success? Why did I think it was selfish to make lots of money? Even though I had been blessed with a best-seller and had earned seven figures I still felt something was missing. I was meeting new people every day; something I always enjoyed doing. I had acquired everything I prayed for and found myself still unhappy. My success had begun to feel more like a burden than a blessing.

When family members contacted me I immediately thought they wanted money. When customers would call and order books from my company I would put the order off until the last minute. *What is wrong with me? What kind of businessperson does not want to fulfill orders that helps make money?* I couldn't understand *me* at first; but then the answers appeared as clear as day. I didn't want to confess to anyone, not even myself that I was good at selling books, but no longer passionate about it. I wanted to write, not sell.

Hard work and talent for getting things done with people had boosted me to the top of the bestseller list. My team and I had created a business we could be proud of. We had developed a great reputation for being efficient, punctual, timely, and professional. We were dedicated to the cause. In our second year of the book business, I was featured in Success Magazine as one of the self-publishing millionaires that did it the good ole-fashion way -- hard work.

When another self-publisher called to congratulate me I was not enthused or felt that I should share in his enthusiasm. I was more concerned with doing a better job at running my new business. Around that same time it became very difficult for me to fall asleep. My soul was restless. I wasn't just an author anymore I was now a self-made publishing company.

I prayed for God to help me find direction, but I didn’t think he was ready to give it to me, so I began writing down ambitious goals for my publishing company hoping they would excite me enough to rejuvenate my desire to be happy. They didn't.

Two years earlier I felt my passion had become as clear as a piece of glass. Through writing and self-publishing, I was able to inspire people to live their dreams. I was able to help others follow their paths toward a direction of happiness and success. I had found what I loved to do and with this passion my God-given talents were revealed, but it still wasn't enough, so I did the only thing I could do. I kept working.

I wrote my third book. It did quite well too. It was printed in several languages, and produced on Audio, but I still wasn't fulfilled. I tried writing the fourth book, but the words simply would not flow. Everything in my mind was telling me that it was time for me to take a new direction, and become a full time writer, but I was afraid to listen. After all; teaching paid the bills. I had benefits: insurance, 401K, dental, medical and a great health plan.

When I finally accepted my fears, understood my frustrations and worked out my confusion I began to make the connections. I finally surrendered my feelings of fear and connected with myself by being honest about what I really wanted despite the fact it would require a major change in my life.

Reconnect with God

I reconnected with God and one by one God connected me with people who would be instrumental in my transition. People opened doors for me to work, write, speak, coach, and appear as a guest, and with this movement I began to host radio and television shows. Magazine editors, television producers and radio broadcasters were calling. By this time I was writing for twelve national magazines and I was finally happy. Very busy, but happy!

Amazingly each of these jobs and the people I met were linked in some way to my writing and publishing endeavors! The connection of events and the direction of each experience were very obvious. The teaching career I once had was also very beneficial to the success of my new venture. Teaching had prepared me to speak in front of thousands of people without fear. It prepared me to be efficient, punctual, timely, professional, and dedicated to the cause. Teaching was an essential part of why my life was going in the direction that it was going. I had been on the right path all along, and now I was headed in a new direction.

Listening to what my life was telling me provided me with the clarity and confidence that I needed to make personal changes without regret. I was ready to meet my challenges head on and I was feeling happier by the moment. I was really moving in the right direction.

Recognize Disconnections and Connections

Have you ever experienced times when you felt distance from GOD, yourself or others? It's that uncomfortable feeling that you can't describe. Maybe you don't quite know how to explain what's happening, but you know for sure that it's happening.

Any time we are disconnected we are left feeling unworthy, unsure, unclear, lost, frustrated, scatter brained, distant, heavy, confused, doubtful, and mentally drained. These same feelings cause us to lose our way, make poor decisions, and give up. It's not a good feeling.

Then there are other times that we have the right connections. We feel worthy, sure, clear, focused and good about ourselves. We're ready for action and we are full of the kind of energy that it takes to get the job done. When we are worthy, we know what we're feeling and we know what we want to do. Sometimes just knowing that we are connected is enough to make us happy. Then we are happy to be reconnected.

These kinds of connections can leave us feeling born again, rejuvenated, alive and revitalized. We feel reassociated to something or someone, joined, whole again, and ready for positive action. Think about it; how do you feel at this moment? What has helped you reconnect? Tweet me your answer @emp55.

Do you feel connected, disconnected or reconnected?

____

____

At what times do you feel the most connected?

____

____

At what times do you feel disconnected?

____

____

At what times do you feel reconnected?

____

____

Your Connections

Life moves us very quickly sometimes, so much so, that we aren't able to control when bad or good things are about to happen to us. We are provided with opportunities and amenities that allow us to have what we want when we want it.

We eat on the run, work on the run, set deadlines on the run, raise our families on the run, worship on the run and we even rest on the run. Because of this 'on the run syndrome' we are in constant overdrive trying to make time for all the things that we need to do to make our lives better.

As we work on our "to do list" it's very difficult to connect on every level. This can cause someone or something to lack its proper attention. Most times it's the people we care about that come up short on our list of to-dos. In these times most of us have families that are mobile and our loved ones are miles away, but even families who live in the same city can be disconnected from one another. It may be because of distance, but most often it's because they are disconnected emotionally, socially, physically or spiritually from one another.

Busy schedules leave little time for nourishing our relationships. Neighbors who live near one another have become distant because there are too many things to do on their faithful to-do-lists. This leaves gaps in the bond. So, for a moment, consider your day-to-day activities and requirements. Are you connected or disconnected from the people you love the most? What has ruined or improved these connections? Tweet me your answer @emp55.

Welcome to the Neighborhood

I was born in St. Louis, Mo. and grew up in East St Louis, Ill. It was considered neighborly to greet new neighbors with a home cooked meal or a welcome desert of some sort. It was a friendly gesture to say, "Welcome to the Neighborhood." It was also customary to go to a new neighbor's home and introduce yourself.

Today, people are too busy and bogged down with daily duties to give a simple, but friendly nod to their neighbors. Those who are willing to extend friendly gestures often feel that they may be over aggressive or intruding on their neighbors. In today's society standing on the corner and mingling with your neighbors might be considered loitering. In the past this was part of connecting with your neighbors

Take note of your own attitude about the people you are mingling with. Do you meet, greet or speak to your neighbors regularly? Are you friendly with the cashier at the local grocery store? Do you make an effort to say hello when you pass neighbors that you live near? Do you say simple hello's with a smile on a regular basis? If not, you might be disconnected? Why don't you begin today improving your connections?

Make Personal Communications

Disconnection is evident in how we communicate day-to-day with other people. With the invention of cell phones, Internet, emails and IPAD'S; our personal communications have been kicked to the curb. With sky high company budgets, cut backs and downsizing we do more voice-to-voice communication than we do face-to-face communications. Simple telephone conversations have been replaced by the Internet; Instagram, Facebook, and Twitter. We might communicate more, but we use less personal communication. It's the new way of our world.

We don't have to see people, shake their hands, see their facial expressions, body language, or experience their human side. We simply do not have to talk to people unless we want to and when we don't want to it's easy to say, *"I was out of touch."* Technology has given us the power to 'communicate conveniently.' Television has proven that people will now look at anything except each other. Technology has somehow replaced good-ole-fashion communication. These are definitely signs of the times.

Are Your Connections Weak?

But how do you know when your connections are weak? Here a few examples of negative connections. They will help you find out if you are disconnected.

- You learn to live with conditions you do not love.
- You learn to love a job you do not appreciate.
- You feel pressure because you are trying your best to live up to others expectations.
- Your life has become boring and routine.
- You feel that there is no true purpose in your life.
- You feel frustrated or bored with your loved ones.
- You regret giving time to loved ones.
- You would rather stay in bed all day, every day.
- You feel that going to church is an obligation.
- You do not pray and try to avoid people that do pray.
- Making decisions is difficult for you.

- You find it difficult to defend yourself.
- You feel alienated from members of your family.
- You feel worthless and unappreciated.
- Your finances are in total chaos.
- Your life is worthless and you don't want to work toward making it better.

Are Your Connections Strong?

When our connections are strong we tend to become knowledgeable and are able to recognize what the right and wrong messages are. We began to understand why our communication skills have valuable powers. Once we decide that we are free to make connections with others and ourselves we can get in tune with the direction our destiny wishes us to take.

When we understand the importance of connections we have a sense of purpose and fulfillment. Here are a few samples of strong connections.

- Your future and your destiny are bright.
- You have a future that allows you to remain hopeful and you believe that anything is possible.

- You thrive on the thought of learning more.
- You seek spiritual growth on a continuous basis.
- You enjoy time with your family and you make the time you spend with your family a wonderful experience.
- You feel a learning experience from every experience.
- Prayer is important and you make an effort to pray daily.
- Your community involvement expresses your values.
- You are confident about making major decisions that impact your life in positive ways.
- You thrive on life and you love to live life.
- Your financial plans reflect your values and visions for a bright future.

Connecting With Your God

We ae all connected to God and one another in our own special way, but one of my favorite bible verses is "Hear me when I call, O God of my righteousness: thou hast enlarged me when I was in distress: have mercy upon me, and hear my prayer." (Psalms 4:1)

God hears our prayers. All we have to do is seek direction in our lives. The first move is ours to make. God's heart is always open to our needs, hoping that we will open our hearts to his. God does not force his way into your life, but if you take action and reach out to him you will begin to experience His divine presence in your life.

It's that simple: with that power your potential for success is possible. All you have to do is approach God with a divine heart and begin to practice spiritual connections on a regular basis, believing that He cares about you, your circumstances and your success.

A great verse in the bible that continues to strengthen our belief system is "O Lord my God, in thee do I put my trust; save me from all them that persecute me and deliver me." This means if we trust in God, He will give us His blessings.

Get In Tune with Your God

When you are in tune with God you are naturally building your spiritual connections and increasing your power to stay connected. Just like a flashlight; when the batteries are full of power, the light is bright and helpful. When the battery begins to run low, the power is reduced and the light burns dim.

When you are cut off from your power source you are no longer able to access what you need to function successfully, therefore you can't get in tune with God if you don't take time to connect. You have to spend some important private time with God in order to build and strengthen your relationship with God. The best connection with God is through prayer and the bible.

Get In Tune with Yourself

Many people don't become successful because they don't know what they want or how to go about getting what they want. They are not in touch with themselves. People feel better when they are accepted, even though it sometimes causes confusion with what they want for themselves.

We want to believe that we are smart enough to make our own decisions, but underneath it all we might believe that someone else is smarter and has a wiser or better answer. Because of this we relinquish our power to them and when we do this we decrease our connection with ourselves.

Messages are often delivered to us from people that we respect and hold dear to our hearts. We usually take someone else's advice because it is right or because we don't trust our own instincts.

If we are not honest with ourselves about what we want, we end up pursuing dreams, relationships and material possessions that have no real meaning and then we find ourselves frustrated, depressed and feeling bad. Our true purpose is found when we learn to connect and get in tune with ourselves.

Dealing with Yourself Honestly

Dee wanted to move up the corporate ladder the quickest way she could. She said she wanted to transition out of her "safe and secure" corporate management position and begin running her part-time consulting business on a full-time basis. For reasons she could not explain, she felt stuck. One major project was three months behind schedule; she could not seem to get caught up. When I asked Dee if she was having the same problem in other areas of her life, her silence was followed by a reluctant admission: Her closets were so cluttered she could not see the floor; her laundry was piled with dirty clothes. She couldn't seem to find the time to complete her tasks, and her boyfriend who she had broken up with was still living with her.

One by one we found more problems that appeared to have nothing to do with her job. Week by week she seemed to make slow and steady progress - she had to finally deal with her issues. It was time for her to deal with her ex-boyfriend, and then she needed to get caught up at work. She had to also deal with the clutter in her home. Once she became unstuck from the clutter, she would have to begin answering questions about her job. At her present job where she was marketing manager, she had realized years ago that she hated marketing and had no desire to create websites for hotels and resorts. Knowing that her Bachelor's degree prepared her to do that, some of her co-workers had advised her to pursue computer technology. They were looking at her past to determine what she should be she should be doing in the future - and she did just that. Have you ever been in a situation like this? How do you feel about your current situation?

"What is it that you do that doesn't feel like work when you are doing it?" I asked Dee this same question.

"I like teaching entrepreneurs how to become travel agents." I even created a business plan that helps people learn how."

Dee's story shows that you can have the answers right in front of you, yet allow your fears to blind you to them. Instead of depending on what has happened in your past or on others for direction - you must be willing to ask yourself the questions that will reveal who you really are and what you really want. Remember that what you have learned in your past can be used as your stepping-stone to a better future.

Honesty is essential for connecting with yourself because genuine connection is based on truth. If you lie to yourself or refuse to hear the truth, it is impossible to find your unique path. The truth may not always be what you want to hear, but when you listen and then work through it - it offers opportunity for tremendous growth.

Why Are You Feeling This Way

When you find that you are acting out or behaving in bad ways you should ask yourself why you're acting like this. Ask yourself what it is that you really want. It is unlikely that you will feel jealous of a lifestyle, position or situation that you don't have in some way desire for yourself. Feelings of jealousy, irritation, anger, sadness, control and manipulation issues can help you discover who you really are. Rather than beat yourself up about these negative responses, ask yourself why you feel the way you feel and why you do the things you do. If you are truthful in your awareness you will likely discover honest answers and gain a new perspective – the kind that will help you move forward and gain control.

Continue to Ask Yourself Pertinent Questions

One of the most popular ways of getting to know yourself is by asking and answering questions that identify what you need and why you need it. "Why" gives your inquiries purpose. Ask yourself, "What is the most important goal for me to accomplish?"

Try to understand that your values represent who you are and what you are about - and they serve as your directional compass. Your values are something you are willing to defend to the end, and they are aligned with the direction you should go.

People who are extraordinarily successful express their values daily through their relationships, work, finances, spiritual life, and physical activities. Your core values are in tune with what God wants you to be. Your values are important and you should not settle for less than what you believe is in tune with your core values. Ask yourself, "What are my core values?" The list below demonstrates core values. Underline the ones that you feel are a reflection of you.

Adventure
Accomplishment
Achievement
Abundance
Affection
Beauty
Community
Creativity
Commitment
Compassion
Courage
Control

Charity
Change
Curiosity
Communication
Dedication
Determination
Empowerment
Education
Energy
Excellence
Freedom
Fairness Fun

Fitness
Family
Growth
Happiness
Humor
Holiness
Health
Integrity
Independence
Integrity
Intellect
Joy

Love
Ministry
Purity
Perfection
Purpose
Preparation
Patience
Partnership
Professionalism
Romance
Role model
Risk
Righteousness
Service
Sensitivity
Sincerity
Security
Strategy
Support
Spontaneity
Truth
Victory
Wealth

Look at your list. Now, from the values you underlined identify the top five that are the most important to you.

1.
2.
3.
4.
5.

From time to time revisit your list as a means of ensuring that the direction you are going is corresponding with what is important to you. We all get off our desired course sometimes and stop moving toward our dreams. Revisiting your list will help you get back on track.

Learning to Bond with Yourself

Who is the one person in this world you love most dearly? Imagine for this moment that you are with this person. What are some of the things you would do together and what are some of the ways you have been there for each other? If you're in a crowded restaurant, a park or a public place how would a stranger look at your relationship with this person and determine how you felt about one another? Do you love yourself as much as you love this person?

To answer these questions, an onlooker would probably consider how the two of you are treating each other; your attentiveness, your connection, your body language, the kinds of things you do for one another and the concern for each other's wellbeing. If you confess your love and acknowledge your love for someone you would not treat him or her badly would you?

Do your actions suggest undying love and dedication to this person or does it show anger, resentment or any other negative signs?

Your answer ____________________________________

Are you honest with your answers? __________________

YES________ NO____________SOMETIMES ___________

I'm sure you've probably heard the saying "Actions speak louder than words." This is the way many people feel about their loving relationships, but not their relationships with themselves. When you love yourself you automatically build better relationships with others. Loving yourself also builds your confidence, courage and self-esteem. It helps you make choices that lead you in the right direction. Loving yourself is the best way to strengthen your acknowledgement of the fact that you are meeting your own needs.

Learning to Love Yourself

Loving relationships helps the love deepen. The same is so when you love yourself. As time passes your acts of love become the foundation of relationships that are solid. This also solidifies your relationship with self. Every time you stand up for yourself you are showing love for yourself. When you take time to pamper yourself you are showing that you love yourself. When you treat yourself with respect and demand others to do the same you show love for yourself. When you take responsibility for eating right and living right you show love for yourself.

Are you in a relationship of love and respect with yourself? Does your attitude display this same kind of relationship? Does your body language display that you care for and love yourself?

Place a checkmark by the statements that are true to you:

_ I place everyone's needs before my needs.

_ I don't say no even when I know I should

_ I make excuses for not pampering myself.

_ If I feel tired I keep going until I am totally exhausted.

_ I put up with rude or inappropriate behavior from others.

_ I feel guilty about things that I do for myself.

_ I hide it when I do good things because I'm afraid people will become jealous of me.

If you checked any of these statements, you have some work to do. There's nothing to be ashamed about, knowing that you have work to do is acceptance of the knowledge you have. If the majority of these statements don't apply to you then you are probably living a good life.

Moving In a Direction of Self-Love

Remember, you want to move in a direction that takes you away from self-neglect and disrespect. This is the only way you will gain self-love, peace and joy. And with all of this you'll begin to enjoy the person you're really meant to be. Nourishing your mind, body and soul means you have more of yourself to deal with in joyful ways. Your love for self will facilitate your connection with self.

Bonding with Other People

Let's test your bonding power with people by answering these questions.

1. How did you get the job you currently have?
2. How did you meet your mate?
3. How did you meet your best girlfriend?
4. How did you meet your best guy friend?
5. How did you start your business career?
6. Why do you remain in the city you live in?
7. What made you move to the city you now live?

Ask Yourself Questions

Do the people you communicate with on a daily basis connect with you effectively? Are they hampering your communications or do they help you move in the direction you would like to move. Most people know that in order to succeed in this world you must have strength in communication and be able to connect with people on all levels.

One of the reasons Oprah Winfrey is so successful - is her ability to communicate with all people on a level that they can understand and comprehend. Her communication skills stretch globally.

Imagine if you were able to communicate on that level. Wouldn't you be considered a phenomenal woman too? Many people are stagnated in the jobs and life they have because they fail to communicate effectively. They don't know how to connect.

Opportunity comes more quickly and often to those who are compassionate, courteous, and easy to get along with. Good 'direction connections' with others might include:

- *Meeting your purpose in life.*

  You should use your God given gifts to serve others in a positive way. Having a positive impact on a life other than your own helps you live with purpose.

- *Learn as much as you can about yourself.*

  Discover your likes and dislikes, your limits and opportunities. What is it that excites you or frustrates you? Do you know? You should consider learning these things.

- *Give love and accept love.*

  Any life is better when love is present. Love helps your life become more fulfilling.

As you find yourself bonding, connecting and communicating with God, others and yourself you should be able to find more opportunities to move in the right direction. This happens when you are actually living the way you are supposed to be living.

When you are living with purpose, when you are walking the walk and talking the talk, you are using your natural gifts and talents and are making an impact on the world. You are living right. Opportunities are abound because you are living a conscious life. As you communicate and contact people who come across your path many of them will be a gift from God to you while in others eye sight you will be their gift from God. Practice giving and receiving is a positive means of healthy communication.

Connect to Your Communication Power

What are your three greatest achievements? List them.

1.
2.
3.

Who helped you connect with your dream?

____

Who urged you to seek out your dream?

____

Who motivated you as you pursued your dream?

____

Now ask yourself what is the most powerful connection that leads you to these people? Try to think back as far as you can. You'll probably find that your best connections can be traced back to only a couple of people.

You might ask why this is an important connection. First, it illustrates why one connection, event or communication can be very important to moving you in the right direction. This helps you also understand that one connection can also make you or break your effort to move forward. Maybe you remember your grandparents saying, *"Don't ever burn a bridge. You may have to cross it one day."* Burning communication bridges not only impacts your situation it also impacts your life negatively.

Having a bad attitude can spiral into a negative reputation with hundreds of important people whom you might need later on in life. Having fallouts with one person earlier in the day could cause you to loose major contracts or business connections later in the week. It could even be damaged with people you have never made contact with. One bad attitude with one person can ruin your reputation later down the road.

The flip side is that there are good sides too. You can have a good attitude with one person that day and find that it has opened many beneficial doors. Think of all the people who have connected with you. Can you honestly say that each experience was a good one? Did each have the potential to help you earn more fortune? The path you take can help you change direction and lead you to a new way of living.

Open Your Eyes So That You Can See

You have to look for opportunities. As you find yourself doing more connecting, bonding and communicating with others ask God for the wisdom to know and understand what your purpose is. You may pray for success, but if you don't know how to go about getting that success you won't recognize valuable resources and opportunities that can help you move to the next level. Praying does help, but knowing what to pray for helps even more. Be prepared to accept changes that may come as you prepare your life for the opportunities that cross your path.

Ask yourself "What are some of the connections I can make that will help improve my life and my situation?"

Are you…..

- Helpful
- Approachable
- Interested in others well-being
- Taking things too personal
- Doing your best at all times
- Seeing the whole situation as it really is
- Respecting others time
- Respecting others resources
- Connecting with God and yourself
- Clear about who you are

Work on Communication Connections

If you want to improve your communication you must learn to connect with others. Disconnection occurs when the lines of communication are weak and filled with unproductive information or there is too little genuine human interaction.

During a communication session with one of my clients Karl, he mentioned an upcoming family gathering that he wasn't going to attend because he and his father were not on speaking terms. This relationship turmoil went as far back as high school, just as Karl was entering into adulthood. As Karl began to make plans for his adult future his father seemed to become very controlling. Perhaps Karl was too young to handle the dynamics of an adult son and father relationship or maybe his father didn't quite know how to hold on to a son who was ready to move on. For whatever reason, the failure in communication resulted in increased tensions and what began as a transition into adulthood snowballed into a ball of anger, resentment and control. Twenty years later the separation was as strong as ever and Karl was reluctant to attend family gatherings for fear of confrontation.

Karl wished and dreamed for a better relationship with his father. It was so emotionally draining to have such a distant relationship from his father, but he was so close to his friends and other family members. This bad relationship with his father was beating him down in more ways than one.

I asked Karl "What do you want to do to improve your relationship with your father?"

He replied, "I'd like to be able to be a part of his life and on the road to communicating with him again. I want us to be close again."

"His answer moved us to find ways that he could take positive action.

"I need to make things right between us; after all he's the only father I have. If something happened to him I could not live in peace." With that said he understood better that he had nothing to lose by opening up to his father, so he did. Today Karl's relationship with his father is steadily improving, but it will take patience on both their parts. The good thing is as Karl works to improve his relationship with his father it will help him get to know himself better and that's why a willingness to connect a little is better than no connection at all.

Communicate Your Purpose

As you move in a more positive direction you'll start to recognize key indicators regarding your purpose in life. When you pursue your purpose you move toward your success. You have life purpose assignments as a part of your movement.

If you are in the teaching profession your life purpose might include educating young adults. If you are a medical doctor your life purpose might include saving lives or even cure people of diseases. Each profession involves encouragement, comfort, or sharing helpful information to others about living a life of purpose.

As you move in the direction that allows you to fulfill your own dreams and help others along the way, other opportunities are sure to arise. As you fill your life purpose assignments you will discover that some of them are more challenging than others. These challenges will help you complete your own life purpose assignments with minimal amount of effort and when you find that some of them take on more effort than you expect you will know that it is a test of your passion for that particular purpose.

During my years of teaching and coaching young adults I was very dedicated to helping them find their own life purpose. We begin with having them assess what is most important to them. We find what they are most passionate about, what their values are and what gets them excited. For a moment recall your own top values. Tweet me your answers @emp55.

List 3 things that you are passionate about.

1.

2.

3.

Your Next Move

Are they a part of your life's passion? What did you learn by examining your values and the things you are passionate about? What does this list reveal about your life's purpose? Why are they important to you? It's sometimes difficult to reveal your purpose in a few words, so I've listed a few examples that should help you understand better how to do it yourself.

- *Denella* desired a career in communications. She wanted to supervise hotel employees in an office of brand communicators. Denella has a personality that inspires others to excel in the communications field. The passion she has shines through in her personal and professional life. The way she lives her life exemplifies her passion to be the best person she can be.

- *Brad* wanted to express his artistic creativity through his paintings and glass designs. He wanted to dedicate his life by helping others learn the importance of using their own creative ability. Through his attitude and the way he lives, he expresses his creativity daily.

- *Dora* wanted to inspire and motivate others to become excellent financial planners. By using her prior work experience she teaches others how to take what they already know and use it to excel their financial status. She helps more people plan for success by investing, saving and spending smarter. She exemplifies her financial planning skills by not only teaching others, but also by doing what she is teaching. She walks the walk and talks the talk. Now you try it.

Helpful Communication Solutions

Your communication is very essential to your success. It reveals what's going on around you and helps you understand other people's motives and needs. Communications increase your learning, therefore making you more competent and more powerful. It can be very helpful in winning the respect and building the esteem of followers who appreciate your attention. It defuses anger by giving others a chance to vent and express themselves verbally and it can be the difference in helping you find out what type of leader you need to be.

When you encounter people who act uninterested in improving their communication or they appear to be resistant to communication here are some simple solutions you can practice.

1. Have an agenda.

   Say exactly what you want to talk about and what you hope to accomplish from the conversation. Give focus and direction to your conversation.

2. Ask questions that interest other people too.

   Don't focus your concerns on things only you are interested in. Involve the other person. Understand others interests and concerns.

3. **Give your partner a chance to communicate.**

   Don't hog the conversation. Allow conversation an equal opportunity. It helps all of those involved to feel like an active part of the conversation.

4. **Don't hint at what you want.**

   It's better to be direct, while communicating. Hinting around at what you want only serves to irritate the person to whom you are hinting or miscommunicating.

5. **Commit to improve your listening.**

   If you aren't already a good listener you're not likely to reform without total commitment. Most deaf ears have to get angry before they really commit to listening.

7. **Limit your talking.**

   You'll never be able to talk or listen at the same time. Be quiet sometimes. Don't your answer while the other person is talking. Take time to respond once the other person is finished talking.

8. **Don't draw conclusions about people and things.**

   Many times we listen to the people that we think are worth listening to. When we listen we often hear what we expect people to say even though they didn't say what we thought we heard. Listen deeper then make a decision about what you heard.

9. **Hold your fire.**

   When others say things that might excite, displease, or trouble you hang onto your emotions until the person that's speaking completes their thought. If you interrupt then, you risk offending, angering or disappointing them. As a result the message is likely to be discarded or distorted.

When you communicate with others try your best to connect and bond before making decisions or placing judgment. Then you can identify the direction your conversation should take.

In the next chapter we will discover the checklists for taking control of your life, which will prepare you to do just that.

Let us make a special effort to stop communicating with each other so that we can have some conversation.

\- Mark Twain

Chapter 9

Mindset 8: Gaining Self-Control

In this chapter you will discover how to take control of your life, move forward and stop blaming yourself for past mistakes.

This Is Your Chance to Make a Difference

J**ust for a moment let's imagine** that this is a chance to make a difference in your own world. Imagine that you are speaking from your soul to chance. Take a look around. Does chance surprise you? You never imagined chance to look like this did you? Chances are you are unaware of your own worth, because your soul has been hidden by chances that are visible for only those who have eyes to see it. Chance can only lead us to our destiny. It is up to us to choose to transform our chance into luck through courage, risks, leaps of faith, ah ha moments and even a few what the hell moments.

Chance is a beautiful thing if we are blessed with the gifts it gives. The boy who found the Dead Sea Scrolls buried in a cave in jars didn't even began to understand their worth; the cobbler who bought the scrolls from him only bought them because he thought they would make strong soles for his shoes. But something stopped him from tearing them apart; instead he scratched the leathery surface and discovered writing on the bottoms. He didn't even know what the writing meant but because he was religious man his spirit encouraged him to dig deeper so he took them to a Syrian confessor. The priest was flabbergasted at the fact that anyone could be wearing the lost Old Testament Book of Isaiah on their feet. This should be our lesson that in our life we can have fortune or loss in the palm of our hands. Chances are this is your chance to get it together.

It's Never Too Late To Get It Together

My mother was sixty-five years old and finally living the life she had dreamed of. She went about her day just like any other workday. She woke up, ate breakfast and went to work on a new project each day. Since all the children were adults and living on their own - she was ready to live her life to the fullest. Mother kept herself busy with her chores and hobbies around her small two bedroom house. There were curtains to be hung, laundry to be done and she needed to get started. Mother tended to all these things and was excited about her entrance into her new life. Little did she know… the unspeakable was about to happen.

Unspeakable Drama Hits My Momma

As my mom prepared for bed later that night she sipped from a glass of milk. Milk was her drink of choice. It was a memorable day for her. She was finally away from the hectic and busy life of all her sons and daughters. She moved from California back to her childhood home of East St Louis and was embarking on a new life. She was happy again, at least until she fell asleep that night.

The stranger woke her up sitting on top of her chest. She could feel his sweaty hand over her mouth and he said, "Don't move or I'll cut your throat." She could remember the stench of liquor on his breath. As he straddled her chest she could feel his weight cutting off her air supply. She gasps for air and he mistook it as her trying to speak. He pulled his private part out and rubbed it against her shaking body. "Don't move, don't scream and I won't hurt you old lady." Then he removed his hand. Mother was sleeping when it all began. She didn't hear him enter her home. That was a terrible night for our family. I will never forget it.

Time didn't dull my mother's recollection of that awful night. She recounts the details of her assault with the kind of precision that would have certainly landed her assailant in jail - if only the police had caught him.

Mom's bedroom was illuminated by the eerie outside light shining in her bedroom. Mother had fallen asleep with her window cracked. It was hot that night and to save on her electricity bill she left her window slightly open. In the wee hours of the morning when the rapist woke her up, all she could feel was a cold object against her neck. He had grabbed mother's cutting shears as his weapon.

He was young - she said - maybe in his early twenties. He felt lighter than her in weight. He felt skinny she said, maybe about 150 pounds. She remembered that his hands were rough and he smelled like alcohol and marijuana. There was no chance of her fighting him off. She just lied there and prayed for him not to kill her. It was a helpless episode, a sickening episode. He raped her as she quietly cried.

He kept repeating obscene gestures and telling her what he was going to do to her. It made the situation all the worst for her. He even told her how he had been watching her for the past week. She thought she was dreaming. He uttered violent and cruel things to her during his violation of her. It lasted no more than ten minutes and she doesn't remember crying aloud. She remembered being so afraid that her stomach felt like it was going to cave in.

After he completed his rape, he grabbed the bedspread from the bed and wiped himself. Them he threw it on top of mother. Before he ran out of the back door he told her not to move and then he was gone. Mother jumped out of the bed and headed for the front door. When she burst out the door there was a car in her front yard that she didn't recognize. It was the assailant's car and someone else was in it with the motor running. He had come to rob her, but noticed her asleep and took advantage of her. My mother ran to her neighbor's house and called the police. She had gotten the first three letters of the truck's license number.

Not Quite the Same Again

The police came, took her to the doctor and then took a police report from her. She flew back to California to stay with my brother and sister for the next four months. I went home to move all her things out. For mother home isn't home anymore, but she misses the place she once called her safe haven.

Physically my mother had healed, but emotionally she would never be the same. She never admitted it, but we all knew that it was too painful for her to discuss with us. She's always considered herself strong, and to be taken advantage of made her feel weak.

She was always playing it safe, but now she has lost her sense of being safe in her own home. We even had to beg her to relocate from this place of pain. She refused. She was going to go back to the place it all happened. Somehow my mother always came out okay. But this time she's different. Throughout the rape this animal described how he had been watching her, so for all she knew he was still somewhere near watching and waiting for a chance to return to her bed.

"There is no way mother will ever be able to let her guard down now. No chance of her ever being the same again." No chances of ever getting pass the pain.

Getting Back To Normal

Wouldn't our lives be perfect if we could get back to the way we once were. Getting our lives back to normal means we should actively work to meet our personal goals. We should be able to create an environment where we can grow safely, professionally and personally. In doing this we can achieve a higher level of success and happiness. Getting past any pains or hardships is sometimes difficult, but we must try. Trying is the first step.

Staying On Top of Your Game

I too had to tighten my game, not like momma, at the same level of importance. I recall the day I met Oprah. That day is still fresh in my mind. I was working out in the gym at the Hotel Bel-Air and noticed her out of the corner of my eye - standing near the exercise machine that I was about to use. I didn't know who she was at first. She was in the corner of the workout room on the telephone. I could tell she was talking business, and I was trying my best not to stare, but I was excited. I was eager to work out because I had some important meetings with television and radio executives later that day and I was so nervous that I wanted to run a little to reduce some of my anxiety. About five minutes later Oprah got on the treadmill next to me and started jogging. As I looked to my left, we caught each other's eye. She was so excited about working out that she was blurting out ... Yes! Yes! Yes! I was excited about being in the same room with her and fought back the urge to yell with her.

I thought, "Now I can tell my friends I worked out with Oprah."

She was talking to herself, saying things like "Yes!" "Go for it" and "You can do it." She was so hyped that I couldn't help but get hyped too. Her energy filled the room. Finally she looked over at the speed I was going on my treadmill and said "Oh come on, if you can go 3.7 miles an hour surely you can go 4.0 miles per hour.

I thought I should be doing a good 3.0. I was really pushing the 3.7 and I was only running that fast because she had hyped me up. With my bad-self I pushed the button up to 4.0 and after about ten seconds I thought I was going to pass out. I was so inspired by Oprah that I felt I could have gone up to 5.0 if I really tried.

When I got back to my room I called my agent who was in another room in the hotel and told her I had just met Oprah, unofficially of course. Then she asked me the infamous question: "Did you tell her about your book?" I could have died. I was so excited about being in Oprah's presence I completely forget to mention my book or give her a book. I was upset with myself for the duration of the trip because I felt like I had missed my chance. My agent was furious to say the least. Anyone in the literary field knows that a chance to talk with Oprah is a good thing, but I wasn't paying attention! Giving her my book might have opened some closed doors for me. I failed to take advantage of a golden opportunity. I wasn't paying attention to the opportunity that was right in my face and I'm still kicking myself for that one. Are there any mishaps in your life that you wish you could take back?

Don't Miss Your Chance

Part of taking control of our lives is being able to recognize our golden moments. With the blink of an eye these moments can be lost. To take control of your life you have to be mindful of golden moments. Being able to develop and separate your positive thoughts from your negative thoughts is part of this achievement. With the correct mindset the value of the possibility for you to succeed should never be underestimated. You can open doors for yourself just by taking control of your moments. You have to stay alert and be ready to make a move. Sometimes taking control of your life can come from pleasantries. You've probably heard of all the negative things that cause people to take control of their lives, but if you take another look at your own life you'll find positive ways to take control. My Oprah moment could have changed the direction of my life. I missed my chance, don't miss yours.

Capitalize On Your Moments

Nothing will work effectively for you unless you learn to take advantage of your opportunities. When you take control of your life, you exemplify your personal leadership abilities and qualities. Being in tune and mentally aware as well as taking control gives you the power to choose your dreams and reach your goals. It helps you capitalize on moments you might otherwise miss.

Don't do as I did: I had the biggest television personality in a room; she and I were working out with no interruptions. We were having pleasant conversation and I failed to take advantage of the prime situation. All I had to do is offer her my book. Even if she didn't like it I could have put it in her hands and who knows she might have read it, liked it and talked about it on her show. Then the rest would have been a phenomenal business adventure. I was so in awe with her that I failed to capitalize on the moment. Big mistake! Yes, big mistake.

To Change You Must Focus

Maybe your life has not been filled with these kinds of missed opportunities or crisis. Maybe you just want to know how to get to a place where you can take control of it. It's difficult sometimes, but you won't be able to change your situation if you don't pay attention. When you run around in a crazy rush, you only create more anxiety. You've got to get control by slowing down that racing motor inside of you. Sometimes you have to relax or take a break just to give your mind more focus.

Don't Confuse Control with Selfishness

Some people confuse taking control of their lives with selfishness. There is a fine line between confidence and taking control because they work hand in hand. We express ourselves, we are the center of attention, we aren't afraid to ask for help and we are equally ready to try to solve problems that may arise. We aren't afraid of rejection and we don't allow the word NO to frighten us. We don't need alcohol or drugs to create our ego. All we need is a healthy, attitude about who we are. We are confident and in control.

Your mind will begin to accept what you program it to think if you repeat the message often enough. It doesn't matter if what you say is true, or if the statements are positive or negative; if you repeat the words often enough, you eventually believe them.

If you recite aloud to yourself on a daily basis, *"I believe in myself,"* and if you recite it with conviction, your mind will believe and accept the statement as fact.

With that said why not start today believing that you are just as capable as anyone else is. Find what your basic needs are for successfully taking control of your life and reaching your personal goals. Why not consider the fourteen principles below as your guide for becoming confident and in control of your life.

14 Mindsets to Help Take Control of Your Life

1. **Don't allow others to control your life.**

   Don't turn your life or assets over to outside forces and don't allow the lack of finances to determine your dreams or goals.

2. **Don't allow facts to control your life.**

   Many problems are created from facts. Sometimes your problems can handicap you into thinking that things are factual so you don't do anything to change or challenge them. Facts often influence people. Decide whether the facts that are presented to you are beneficial or harmful. Don't allow facts to defeat or change your positive outlook on life.

3. **Don't allow body language to control your life.**

   Body language can indicate support or lack of support from the people listening to you. If you see eyebrows raise or hear people swallow loudly as you are presenting an idea, you might begin to feel agitated or unsure. Don't let others impressions of you make you feel less than who you are.

4. **Don't allow lies to control your life.**

   Lies are the masks of negative thoughts. Don't become a part of this belittlement. Don't live with lies that control your views. If you tell one lie most likely you'll have to tell another one to keep things straight. It's not worth the stress.

5. **Don't allow frustrations to control your life.**

   If you begin to feel that you can't handle people, or problems associated with your life, you are only giving in to the frustrations in your life. When you began to feel frustrated try to refocus and work on solving your problem instead.

6. Don't allow fantasies to control your life.

Don't allow yourself to be sucked in by elaborate fantasies. Dreams are bigger and better than each of us, so set goals that help your fantasies remain intact.

7. Don't allow fears or failure to control your life.

Fear within comes from you. It's no fun to fail, but if you experience failure, pick yourself up and get back in the race. Remember you have to constantly challenge yourself if you want to be better. In life there are challenges and failure is bound to creep its ugly head in. Persevere and keep it moving.

8. Don't allow fatigue to control your life.

We all get tired from time to time. When you see that you are running tired, back off, sit down, rest a short while. Evaluate the situation and then get back up to fight some more. Plan mini-vacations to unwind, and rejuvenate your mind and body. A few restful hours are all that's needed. Take a break, regroup and hang in there.

9. Don't allow forecasts to control your life.

People who claim to know the outcome of the future or give forecasts on your future tend to help you think negative thoughts. Their purpose is to feed off of your weaknesses and make you feel you need them in order to succeed. Nothing is impossible if you stay in control of your own abilities.

10. Don't allow wild situations to control your life.

When people are confronted with situations that cause panic, they have a tendency to be controlled by their emotions. This is a problem for most people no matter how smart or how successful they are. When you encounter frantic situations, take a moment to just think things through.

11. Don't allow fate to control your life.

Astrology, psychics and social structures have been known to control people. Many people allow their futures to be determined by fate. Chart readers, fortune-tellers and other programs create negative self-fulfilling prophecies. Never let people who claim to know your fate control your life.

12. Don't allow enemies to control your life.

Opposition can create self-doubt or emotional turmoil. Don't allow enemies to take over your life. Your enemies are not interested in solving your problems; they want to make your life miserable. Don't give them the upper hand.

13. Don't allow your friends to control your life.

Some of your friends will be the very people who work against your ideas to succeed. They can give advice, but try not to let them have the final word on your life decisions. Be true to your decisions and you'll be true to yourself.

14. Do allow your life to be controlled by FAITH!

Decide what decisions to make and once you do - take action. Allow your positive abilities to help set your goals. Open your eyes, heart, and soul. Have faith in your decisions. DO believe and DO have faith!

A Moving Thought

You have to know yourself. You will never know who you are or what you want in life until you know yourself.

A Moving Thought

The purpose of life is not to be happy – but to matter,
to be productive, to be useful, to have it make
some difference that you have lived at all.

- Leo Rosten, American teacher and humorist

Chapter 10

Mindset 9: Don't Be Afraid to Believe

In this chapter you'll learn who you are and are able to make the transition from who you are into the person you want to be.

Who Are You and What Do You Want?

By now you should be able to answer a few questions: "Who am I?" "What do I really want out of life?" "What are my expectations and how am I going to achieve what I want?" "Am I the kind of person people love for who I am, or do they expect something from me?"

Many people are dumbfounded when they have to answers questions about their life and the direction they are going or the roads they are not taking. It can be quite overwhelming if things are not the way they want them to be. These same questions can confuse people and make them angry. If we answer these questions honestly we will find that there are people in our lives that appreciate us for what we have accomplished and there are people who appreciate us for what we have. Of course we want everyone to like us for who we are, not for what we have or have accomplished, but life isn't perfect.

Now, let's look at one of these same questions in reverse…

- "Have you accepted people into your life because of who they are or for what they have accomplished?"
- "Do you find yourself unhappy and frustrated for attracting people who are more enamored with image and achievements rather than substance and character?"

You may not want me to ask these questions, but if you use these questions as your catalyst for becoming the person you truly want to be and for getting what you really want in life they could quite possibly lead you to the rewards of moving in the direction that is right and successful for you.

As you began to get comfortable with answering more questions about whom you are and what you want in life you will become intrigued, and enlightened by your own responses. It can be a life altering experience that can transform you into a better person.

Transforming Yourself

As the manager of your life you are also the author of your own life story and responsible for your own success. This might sound a little scary at first, but don't fret because it's normal to be afraid of things you aren't accustomed to. You'll be okay as time goes by.

Think of how unsure you felt when you first opened this book. Since then, you have discovered the positive and loving side of yourself. As soon as you began recovering your lost self you can overcome any negative voice that surrounds your positive one.

Many people make their marks in life later because they decide late in life what they want to do. In your own way you can do whatever it is you've always wanted to do, no matter what your circumstances. You can do exactly what others have done... succeed.

There are hundreds of thousands of people and some you know who felt they were blindly walking through life, letting others decide what it is they should be doing and deciding for them who they should be.

Many of these same people have now become high spirited and determined that they are going to do everything needed to get what they want in life. They have hopes for a future that's exciting and successful.

Getting Accustomed to Success

As a part of your transformation begin learning how to speak the language of success. Find experts that you can pattern your actions after and fully immerse yourself in their culture of success. Study people who speak naturally of million dollar deals. Bring successful conversation's to the forefront of your mind and talk the talk so that you will soon be able to walk the walk. Plan on seeing, hearing and being a part of the next big thing. Fill your speech and any statements you make with the "I am than I am not." I can rather than I can't" and "I will rather than I can't" Attend success driven events and watch your mentors and note how they made it to the top and before you know it you'll be telling others how you made it to the top.

Why are we striving to make it to the top share your inner most secrets with a trusted friend or family member and be sure to keep some things secret sharing only with God and yourself.

Brandi's Issues

My friend, Brandi has been going through lots of personal and emotional issues. She discovered through a routine check-up that she had high blood pressure. Her father who lived with her was diagnosed with cancer and had been given a very short time to live.

Her mother was anemic and Brandi was also in jeopardy of losing her job. Because of her problems she's stopped thinking there was a better life and existence for her. She even stopped dreaming. Brandi interprets her dreams as nightmares.

When I met Brandi she was just like most women I know; hard working, single, and dedicated to her family, but she was also down on herself; feeling inadequate and thinking the only thing she needed to do was care for others. Brandi has no children but gives all of her time to family, friends and other people's children.

On weekends, if she isn't grading papers or running errands for family members she's sitting at home watching television or cleaning what she had already cleaned twice before. She doesn't call her friends because she doesn't want them to know how incomplete her life is.

One day Brandi called me to discuss her problems. I asked her "why, now; have you decided to do something to improve how you feel about yourself?"

"Ella," she told me, "I have so many reasons to live. I want to do more with my life. I've always thought that working for others would be all I needed, but I want more, I need more, so now I want to try to find a way to live my life in better ways." With that one statement, Brandi has turned her life in a different direction. All it took was her decision to do so. In her spare time she began to sell nutrition products. Her first clients were her ailing mother, her father, a few pro athletes and other people whom she was convince needed better and healthier nutrition in their lives. She came in contact with almost everyone she knew when she started selling her products. At least this project motivated her to get up and get out of the house.

She's beginning to feel better about herself and her life. Her attitude has changed, her spirits are high and her life is moving in directions that she's proud to talk about. Because Brandi has finally decided to do something about her life she feels empowered. Her confidence has flourished and her problems have diminished. She found out that it's impossible to feel bad or discouraged for long periods of time if she's moving in positive and fulfilling directions.

Moving Toward Your Dreams

Let's think about this for a minute, if we move toward our dreams our focus can keep us energized, enthused and hopeful. When we continue to dream we move forward. Just like Brandi, we become success and happiness magnets. Moving toward our dreams causes good things to drop into our laps regularly.

Our dreams have a natural way of being completed and they have a way of helping us enjoy the gifts and fruits of life. With all this movement toward our dreams – great opportunities are created.

So many people don't get the chance to enjoy the fruits of life because they are afraid to move toward their dreams. You waste time when you keeping speaking of your dreams and aspirations to people who don't truly understand your wishes. I meet many people who tell me "I have a story to tell, One day I'm going to write a book." I always give the same statement..."Get to writing, and then I ask, "Why aren't you writing?" If you are committed to writing your story then you need to claim the dream as yours.

You will miss out on your true blessing if you don't accept it as yours by claiming it wholeheartedly. All you have to do is commit to the commitment, which I'll speak more about later in this book. Once you commit to your dreams all the other parts of it - the connections, the money, the opportunities and the lifestyle will start coming to you in more ways than one. When you put your efforts into your God given gifts and you make your dreams a part of this gift God will bless you for your efforts. Part of that blessing is to succeed.

Because Brandi is finally able to focus on what she really wants to do, she has begun to believe in herself and has developed skills she never knew she had. She is using her God given talents to live her dreams. She has found herself happier than she's ever been. She is now managing large groups of people and making large sums of money and her health has greatly improved because now she's happy. Brandi's story is a modern success story because she's made dramatic changes in her life despite the cards once being stacked against her. You go Brandi!

Power Comes When Thinking Is Shifted

Now, for a moment, think about your own life and story. Do you feel like your real power comes when you go for what you want? When you are trying to fulfill your dreams does it make your hard work worth it? The power of your dreams can bring you the happiness you desire. No one will ever be able to think, do, and see all things the way you do. If you don't go after your dreams, you will lose valuable treasures. By not going after your dreams you lead a life without challenge or aspirations. Life is too important, valuable and precious to get caught going in the wrong direction; a direction that someone else chooses for you. There are no promises or guarantees that your road will be smooth, your life will be easy, or you'll be free from pain, but as you move in the right direction you will gain a great amount of focus.

By getting a handle on life you can create a plan of action that works for you and creates a path of success so that your dreams will come true. When you feel that you are thinking less of yourself recite this aloud... *"Self were in this together."* And then recite it again.

It's easy to bemoan the lack of attention or material things you didn't get as a child. It's easier to make excuses for yourself based on some injustice - real or imagined - you were forced to endure as a child. The fact of the matter is what's done is done. While you cannot go back in time and undo the suffering - you can do something today to start the healing. Too many of us sit around giving too much of our energy to the past. That's not the way to live life. Starting right here and now, you can shift your thinking, even if it's the same mind set you have carried throughout your entire life. What your parents or childhood did not give you; you should give yourself. The way to start is by remapping your state of consciousness. Many of us, me included have been conditioned to look for approval from the outside. And while I think it's great to have adults in a home that was rich in affirmations, even I have come to grips with the fact that everyone is not rooting for me.

Does any of this sound familiar to you? If so, you are in need of your own inner discovery. Knowing your inner shortcomings is good, but failing to do something about it only continues the cycle of blame games.

Instead of blaming someone else for your problems why not work from where you are right now and then determine how to go about getting what you really want in life.

Are you:

- Capable of doing a lot more than what you're doing?
- Frustrated by your position in life?
- Bored with your life?
- Stuck in your comfort zone - unwilling to take the big risk that will likely catapult you to where you want to be?
- Are hoping that your life will suddenly change and everything you ever wanted will fall in your lap?
- What's stopping you from getting further in life?

Think about these questions honestly and if the answers displease you begin planning a way to bring the answers that you desire.

Knowing What You Want

The best answers to our questions always come when we pose questions that get to the core of an issue. Questioning oneself for the purpose of personal and spiritual growth is what most people would call "Getting to know-self." This getting to know-self mindset provides you with the tools you need in order to address the fears, distractions and challenges that threaten and divert you away from success. Getting to know yourself challenges your beliefs and negative mindsets, help you identify the annoyance that drains you of your energy. It gives you the insight to recognize and avoid the distractions that can lure you onto a less fulfilling path.

If bonding places you correctly on your path, getting to know yourself minimizes the personal obstacles in your way. Some trials and tribulations will of course be beyond your control. You won't be able to stop every pitfall from happening like … that infamous career change, a loved one loss of life, or a financial pitfall. Many challenges, however, are within your control and can be overcome through changing your environment, thinking, and your approach. But before you can resolve each issue you have to employ this 'getting to know-self-concept. For the purpose of this book we will refer to it more deeply as self-evaluation. It will help us get to the root of the problem.

Through self-evaluation you learn from your mistakes, you learn to deal with envy, happiness, and disappointments. Over time issues that once seemed instrumental will become stepping-stones to success. Rather than running from your problems you learn to face them head on and say, "You know what? I have caused turmoil in my life too long. I'm fed up with my joy and happiness being taken. "It's time to let go." "It's time to move forward." “It’s time to move in a better direction.

You can only grow when you are able to question your own actions, noting your intentions and seeking your healthiest mental, spiritual and emotional state of mind.

One of the greatest spiritual truths is that we are not simply having a spiritual experience rather we are having a human experience. Consider how we are each our own unique spirit. Even though we refer to ourselves or identify others by hair color, eye color, skin color, height and weight -- that is only a description of our outer selves.

Our spirit can be described as our entire self. Our spirit is the only part of us that we have held throughout our lives. Think about it for a moment… your face, skin, eyes, nose, and social status may change or leave you, but your spirit stays with you. You are the same person you were born to be. If you lack the courage to transform, the fears and quirks that controlled you yesterday will continue to control you and your entire life. Transformation occurs when you choose to practice healthy self-evaluation, make the changes that needed and then work to improve in those areas that needed changing.

Self-evaluation stirs up many feelings; one day you will feel enthusiastic about the answers to questions you've asked yourself and sometimes you will feel hurt, sadness or even pain from questions that you ask. At other times you will feel excitement and happiness and your spirit will shout enthusiastically…"Yes, I get it." Self-evaluation is powerful and as precious as birth. It's a beautiful experience, filled with pain and glory, and the end result is positive life altering and life changing experiences.

Ask Yourself the Right Questions

The following are self-evaluation questions you should ask.

1. **Ask yourself expand your mind questions.**

   These questions are designed to expand your thoughts beyond your present experiences. They challenge you to see the entire picture. For example, how would it feel to earn large amounts of money... amounts that exceed what you already earn by five times? In what ways are you willing to change to make that happen? - To have the kind of life you've dreamed of what ways would you have to change?

2. **Ask yourself probing questions.**

   Probing questions help you understand the reasons for your actions and reactions along your journey. You ask yourself, "Why I acted or reacted a certain way?" "Why am I afraid?" "What do I want or why do I want this or that?" The purposes of these probing questions are to explore your feelings and provide information that will empower you to change your thoughts and ultimately your actions. Self-evaluation is used to gather information, not to judge or hurt your feelings.

3. **Ask yourself call to action questions.**

   These questions challenge you to move forward or make a positive move in the right direction. "What are you going to do about it?" "What is your next step?" "When is the deadline?" If you don't take action there's no point in asking yourself these questions.

As your spirit moves you in the right direction more questions that only you will know the answers will come to you. Write them down. Answer them. Embrace self-evaluation and be ready to open your mind to the transformation. Here are some symptoms of failing to practice self-evaluation. What are your symptoms saying about self-evaluation?

- You have allowed fear or distraction to keep you from moving in the direction that leads you to your destiny.
- Your challenges repeatedly pressure you. Vicious cycles are a part of your everyday life. (Example: Yo-yo dieting.)
- The fears that are keeping you stuck in the same old places are difficult to change so you don't change.

- You have not identified the obstacles that hold you back.
- You have not embraced new beliefs based on truth.
- You completely ignore bad mindsets that are sabotaging your health, your success and your life.
- You make excuses for not changing. (Example: not enough time, money, education, and skills instead of taking action.)
- You give up too soon when faced with obstacles.
- You desire no growth or your direction is not expanding into a success worthy journey.

Bring Belief Into Your Daily Routine?

- You begin to solve your problems.
- You are compelled to be honest with yourself because you know that honesty is the only real basis for lasting change.
- You move in the right direction at a faster pace.
- You allow time for self-evaluation and self-reflection.
- You accept the truth even when it's unflattering or painful.
- You work daily to clear you path so that you smoothly move in the right direction for success.
- You raise your standards you move in the right direction.

Be Clear About Your Vision

One of the biggest mistakes people make is having big dreams and no goals or visions to make those dreams come to life. Your dreams and vision drives you to make things happen. You imagination is as big as the sky and we all know that the sky is the limit. Your future is now and you won't gain what you want until you change your focus and elevate your commitment. Do not allow your current life to define your future life. Gain a clear vision of what you want your life to be and get into action making it happen the way you want it to be.

Recognize What You Are Feeling

Many of us are afraid of our feelings because we've been taught to hide and ignore them. Others of us allow our emotions to prioritize our lives ultimately controlling our decisions and sometimes destroying our relationships.

When you adopt a healthy attitude toward your emotions, you won't ignore them, nor will you allow them to control you; instead you'll try to learn from them. Recognizing your feelings enables you to listen to your feeling and interpret what your feelings are trying to tell you. Negative feelings are indicators that something is wrong or needs changing.

When you are feeling frustrated about something; that's not working you need to make a change. Instead of focusing on the frustrations you're feeling; try to work things out by coming up with practical solutions to omit problems. Finding solutions will help you uncover the problem and eliminate undo frustration. Revisit why you are feeling the way you feel and then think of ways to change how you are feeling.

Whether you decide to remain frustrated or find a solution to the problem that's causing the frustration is the difference in discovering the truth and steering toward better feelings. What you’re feeling impacts most-all areas of your life. Consider the following emotions when trying to determine a starting point for what are you feeling?

*Hurt
*Loss
*Fear
*Anxiety
*Anger
*Guilt
*Frustration
*Disappointment
*Embarrassment
*Uneasiness
*Overload
*Unworthiness
*Loneliness
*Regret
*Overwhelmed

Waiting to fix how you feel is not an option. The perfect time and season might not ever come. There is no better time than right now to begin pointing your life in a new direction. To help guide and determine what you want - consider the lists that follow:

1. Choose to understand your interests, values and abilities. Focus on and see yourself the way you want to be.
2. Choose to create images. Use your inner wisdom to guide your vision - your vision is going to be more of a discovery than a creation. Take whatever time you need - this is your life, you are now creating your future.
3. Choose to be explicit! Write down the traits you admire most in others?
4. Choose to be realistic! What can you do right now to act more like the person you want to be?
5. Choose to be creative! What are the qualities you would want most that will create the perfect you?

Connect With Other Movers

I have been associated with movers and shakers all my life, but I had no idea they were there to help me find my way. There have been people who fueled me and kept me going in the right direction. Those times that I took the wrong path was great for teaching me valuable lessons. I began connecting with visionaries when I wrote my first book.

It was on a late Saturday night when I met Steve Harvey at his Dallas Comedy Club. He was performing that night and I had made it up in my mind that Steve was going to get an autographed copy of my first book. I had several hundred copies in the trunk of my car at all times. On the night of the comedy show my husband and I arrived a little earlier than the start of the show. As my we got out of the car I rushed to the trunk to grab a book. He asked what was I getting a book for and I told him that it was for Steve Harvey. Steve didn't know me and I didn't know him, but I knew one thing… I was going to do whatever it took to make sure he got my book. When Steve stepped on stage to perform he had my book in his hand and I was excited. Part of his performance included my book content and the audience loved it. I sold over 200 books that night thanks to Steve Harvey's pitch about my book contents.

After that night of selling books people were calling and books were being ordered and sold and I was on my way to the next level. By the end of the week I had sold over 4500 books. Thank you Steve! I've only spoke to Steve once since that night on 1995 and it was in 2013 that we spoke again and he was asking me about how to go about writing his book. I never told Steve that he helped me get my book out to the public. I don't think that throughout our conversation that he knew who I was. I don’t think that he remembers me. It’s been a long time ago that we met.

I made the connection with Steve when we were both struggling to live our dream. He was an up and coming comic and I was an up and coming writer. Steve has passed me up because I slowed down to raise a family, but now I'm on track again and helping others has been my vision.

As Steve has climbed his success ladder I have watched and as I have climbed mine others have watched. Watching Steve has changed my life. Speaking with him reignited my vision and brought my dreams back to the forefront of my mind and helped me keep my own dreams alive. Knowing and other movers really can help you stay focused.

Finding the Correct Answers

As you concentrate on your personal and spiritual growth you may feel pressured to come up with the right answers to your questions. You may be tempted to give wrong answers to these questions, just remember the questions you ask yourself are going to come from the truest part of your soul. Only through honest exploration can you experience pure ‘light-bulb’ moments. When you experience ‘light-bulb’ moments or as some say 'enlightenment' you can safely say you are ready to do the things that will help you live the life you really want. If you are honest with yourself these moments will arrive where there was once darkness, confusion, and bewilderment.

As you learn to explore you engage in self-evaluation, you love yourself and you desire to explore who you are and what you really want. You begin to move confidently, joyfully, and boldly into your own unique path. Through knowledge, prayer and meditation you can travel the right path. It's time to focus on the growth you experience as you get to a place in your life that helps you consistently move forward in the best way possible.

As you begin to evaluate yourself and answer life's questions with honesty you also appreciate your own humanity. Your light bulb moments will scream out "So this is the lesson I was supposed to learn. So, this is what living life is all about."

You suddenly realize that learning, growing and moving in the right direction becomes better and smoother and you now serve the world with purpose. With growth you begin to see how everything in your life fits together perfectly - both the good and the bad. You begin to notice patterns that are healthy and problems that are systematic. Now you know that your problems have a purpose in your life that helps you appreciate your own humanity. Decisions become easier and less intimidating, and it's okay to explore your thoughts and feelings without any expectations of commitment. I know it's difficult sometimes so to help you on your path here are four important tips to guide you in the right direction.

Getting What You Really Want

I could have never made it on my own. Inspiration and motivation has come from so many people and I suppose you have needed them for other things as well. Whatever it is that you want in this life you have to ask for it. I was always so full of hope that I felt my day would come so I never had to ask. In fact what encouraged me to begin asking for what I want is that so many people were offering me help before I even asked. This made me say' nothing beats a failure but a try', so I started asking for help. Successful people who knew were willing to help me and were quite delighted when I asked them for assistance. I felt so dumbfounded... all I had to do was ask. People were ready, willing and able to have a conversation with me. They really and truly wanted to help me. Jan Miller-Rich talks with me. Steve Harvey talked with me. Les Brown talked with me. Gladys Knight talked with me. Sinbad talked with me. Tom Joyner talked with me. Susan Taylor talked with me. Susan DE Passé talked with me. Oprah Winfrey talked with me. I almost missed my opportunities, but still the conversations were all lessons in learning. I got the lessons.

Speaking with other movers helps expand your vision and helps you see it more naturally as something that can happen for you. Speaking with movers is probably just what you needed and what they were looking for. Talk to your visionaries, learn as much as you can and keep it in perspective. They'll enjoy speaking with you. Here are four surefire ways to get closer to the things that you want

1. **Handle today and your future.**

   Remember how you handled your problems in the past and refuse to handle situations in that way. See, feel and hear yourself handling the problem easily. Repetition will guide and help you create a plan to deal with the challenges you face. Jot down on a piece of paper at least three ways you can change your perception or how you communicate your feelings, needs or actions toward a particular situation.

2. **Get joyful and excited about taking action.**

   Appreciate your determination to get what you want in life. Identify what you are really feeling instead of fighting it. Figure out how to turn your life around by associating your life with happier times. Get excited about the idea of turning your life around. Don't allow anyone to take your excitement away. You can handle whatever comes your way by taking action right away. New distinctions will change the way you feel at any time you need to change your emotions in the future.

3. Identify what you are really feeling.

Instead of feeling overloaded step back and ask yourself, *"How am I feeling at this moment?"* By identifying how you are feeling you can transform any feelings into feelings that you desire to feel. You do have the power to immediately change how you feel. As soon as you notice it and decide you're not feeling the way you want to feel.

4. Learn to meditate.

Taking time to sit in silent meditation each day can help you develop focus – and discover purpose – in life. Find a quiet, comfortable spot where you won't be interrupted. Sit in your favorite chair, on a porch swing, on a large rock by a river, lie back in a warm bath if you'd like, or on a blanket on the grass. If your eyes are open, focus softly on whatever are a few feet in front of you. Be still for a few minutes. Enjoy being with yourself. Concentrate on your breathing – slowly breathing in and breathing out. When your mind wanders, notice your thoughts – don't judge them – just let go. That's meditation - being there with self, getting to know your own mind.

Belief Questions

Your Spiritual Health

1. How am I fulfilling my life's purpose? What more do I want to do to fulfill my calling during my lifetime?

   ____

   ____

2. What frustrations have I experienced recently in my life?

   ____

   ____

3. What frustrations am I angry with God about? When did I become angry? Why did it make me angry with God?

   ____

   ____

4. What are the things I am most grateful for? How have these things helped me in my life?

   ____

   ____

5. What were the last three things I experienced anger, frustration or disappointment about?

   ____

   ____

6. How can I replace any negative attitudes I am feeling with forgiveness and love?

____

____

7. What desires would I most like God to help fulfill in my life? How can I exemplify patience while God responds to my desires?

____

____

8. How could my relationship with God help me in these areas?

____

____

From the following list circle the areas that you find frustration and difficulty with.

Forgiveness	Arrogance	Emotional
Controlled issues	Fear	Stability
Bitterness	Self-care	Temper
Pride	Worry	Overeating
Promiscuity	Laziness	Sexuality
Envy	Self-esteem	Hatred
Anger	Patience	Over spending
Lying	Self-control	Acceptance
Trust	Confidence	Jealousy
Lying	Gambling	
Doubt	Temper	

____

Your Physical Health

1. What actions can I take to take better care of my health?

   ____

   ____

2. What emotions do I feel when I put myself first?

   ____

   ____

3. When is my next complete medical examination scheduled?

   ____

   ____

4. When do I indulge in unhealthiest eating mindsets? Why?

   ____

   ____

5. What mindsets are bringing more negatives into my life? What can I do to make a change for the better?

   ____

   ____

6. How do I feel when I am alone in complete peace and quiet? Am I comfortable or uncomfortable? Do I turn the television or radio on? Do I call friends?

   ____

   ____

7. What is it that bothers me most about my mindsets that cause problems with my health? What can I do to change these poor mindsets?

____

____

Keep Moving Forward

I hope you felt something move inside of you as you answered the questions in this chapter. Perhaps they provoked thought, excitement, and anticipation of your possibilities. These questions can serve as your constant tool for self-improvement. Feel free to use them anytime you want. As you make your move in the right direction ask more questions - questions that only you could know to ask. The answers will come. Use your power to communicate and allow the truth of your answers to stimulate your brain about how and when to move forward.

Any information you gather through self-evaluation can help you determine which areas of your life need your attention right now and which areas can create an action plan for meaningful changes in your life. As you continue to employ this forward moving mindset your personal and spiritual growth will remain at the forefront of your mind. You will learn to fearlessly challenge yourself as you stretch beyond your comfort zone and live more fully day-by-day. Remember that even if you have to take small baby steps. Any step is better than no steps.

Ask yourself from time to time, "Am I moving forward?" If you are not then you should be smart enough to know that it's time to make the forward moving adjustment. Do something every day that will improve your life and lifestyle.

We all have setbacks in our yesterdays, but your past doesn't define your future. Today is a new day, you may slip, but God isn't going to let you fall. His loving arms will ALWAYS be there to catch you and put you in a right direction

A Moving Thought

There's some real dark days where you just feel like the story is falling apart in every one. Just keep moving forward, even when you are bluffing, even when you don't quite know what is going to happen next.

- Dan Scanlon

Chapter 11

Mindset 10: Renewing Positive Relationships

In this chapter you will learn how to build healthy relationships, trust others, and do what it takes to earn their trust in you.

Trusting Your Instincts

So far, we've seen how Moving In The Right Direction and setting goals can help anyone achieve the success they desire. We all have a tendency to be comfortable operating within the boundaries we set for ourselves. This helps us feel a sense of control over just about every situation we're in.

Many of us would like to know the purpose of our relationships before we get involved in them. Most of us want to have better relationships don't we? Only the incredibly bright or the incredibly lucky both - can achieve lasting success in today's complex interdependent society. We learn by working with others, and we leverage our capability by forming relationships with those whose skills and attitudes complement our own. When the right combination of people work toward common goals the results are phenomenal.

Knowing Where People Fit In Your Life

As you consider the following questions remember that the people in your life can fit into more than one category. What categories on the following list represent the people in your life?

- Immediate family (parents, children, spouse, siblings)
- Family (includes everyone you are related to)
- Loved ones (may include friends whom you love or who are like family to you)
- Friends (associates at work that you do things with)
- Acquaintances
- Colleagues and coworkers
- Clients and customers
- Neighbors or fellow citizens

Answer the following questions.

1. Who would you like to build a stronger and better relationship with during the upcoming year? How might this relationship differ from other relationships you already have? How will this relationship enrich your life?

   ____

   ____

   ____

2. In your marriage or intimate relationship what is the one thing that makes your mate feel loved? What is the one thing that makes you feel loved?

   ____

   ____

   ____

3. If you are not involved in an intimate relationship what are the five most important qualities you look for in a mate? Do you present the same qualities?

   ____

   ____

   ____

4. Are you asking your mate to be and do things that are difficult for you to do? Are your requests equally fair?

____

____

____

____

5. What are the three most important people in your life? Is there a conflict or problem that needs to be resolved in any of these relationships? If so, what are the first steps you could take to resolve this?

____

____

____

6. What payoffs are you receiving for remaining in a relationship that is not working?

____

____

____

7. What are you afraid of or what is it that you think that people will find out about you?

____

____

____

8. What person in your life loves you for who you are? Who in your life is more impressed with what you do, or how many accomplishments you've made? How do you feel about it?

____

____

____

Solutions to Relationship Problems

Are you making any relationship mistakes that *you* can change? Take a look at the 3 most common relationship mistakes listed below and then review the solutions.

- **We are vague in requests for communication.**

  We often encounter problems because our communications are unfocused and left open-ended. Give your partner direction or develop boundaries in which quality discussion can take place.

- **We can't figure out what he/she wants or needs.**

  This makes us feel out of control or uninformed. We then began to make awkward demands that make our partner feel pressured. Letting your partner know the mindsets in advance - before fear sets in creates more certainty.

- **We need structure in our lives to feel whole.**

  We feel the need to know where we are going in each conversation, yet many of us don't necessary need this type of structure because we like communicating with people in general. Confident people talk without worrying where the conversation is going. They enjoy expressing themselves, and they like listening to others express themselves. Once you get rid of the hidden agenda's in relationships they soon began to flow like melted ice cream: smoothly and without pressing or pushing too hard.

Building Relationships of Trust

There is nothing magical about the process of building relationships, they all take time, effort, understanding and balance. While working with others is good, there are also risks. I have been in situations where people have made assumptions about my goals and visions based on their own wants and needs. And then there have been others who rejected me because I didn't ask for what I wanted. All of these responses given to me by others had me suspicious and unable to trust my own instincts about what was best for me. When you meet with people just because you want or need something they can see its falseness before you ask for anything. They can see through the façade and know the intentions are unworthy.

When you know what you want you can get it because you have nurtured those relationships that will help you succeed. These kinds of relationships require a steady and open level of honesty and openness. When we are trying to meet the demands of breaking new ground, starting a business, interacting with funder of your business or get a raise a nurtured relationship can make all the difference in the world. Building your relationships come from nurturing the relationships but when people decide that they want to be a part of your vision they are actually assessing what they think of you, the risk involved and their potential return.

Your individual style will shine through when you are sincerely interested in people and their growth. In order to build successful relationships you must be willing to change. Here are 24 wonderful principles that will help you build relationships of trust and respect.

1. You deserve friendship and respect.

Building better relationships helps you understand that you are worthy of trust, respect, and friendship from others.

Whatever opinion you hold of yourself, you are entitled to fairness from others. Don't give so much of yourself that your self-acceptance is based on others acceptance of you.

2. Most people are good.

We must understand and accept the idea that most people are inherently good. To prove goodness, all one has to do is go to the source of human life. Look into the eyes of an infant. There seems to be purity, joy, brightness, splendor, sparkle, marvel, and happiness - you know: "good." We learn bad behavior the same way we learn good behavior by observation and experience. The best mindset is to assume people are decent until they prove otherwise.

3. Others like to help you.

Most people like to help others, but are reluctant to offer this help because they don't wish to impose themselves or they simply fear rejection. The mere act of asking for assistance breaks down barriers. Some people find helping others so rewarding they make a career of it, they become teachers, ministers, counselors and other caretakers.

4. Trust is essential.

Some of the most successful relationships are based on

trust. A relationship is doomed to fail when those involved do not trust each other. Trusting others is not an easy thing to do. Trust saves a great deal of time and emotional capital. Both are essential to a growing and aspiring relationship.

5. **Healthy relationships are important.**

   A relationship is not healthy unless it is healthy for everyone involved. It doesn't matter if it is an emotional commitment between two people or an alliance between nations; every participant must receive and perceive equal benefits from it.

6. **Become honest and candid.**

   You can't earn the respect of anyone if you are deceitful or if people suspect you to be taking advantage of them. Don't get off on conceit and dishonesty just to have things your way because no matter what, your dishonesty will show through in the long run.

7. **Become sincere when dealing with people.**

   Do not take bribes or force friendships or relationships. When you force relationships through bribery or insincere means your friendship will soon sour and you'll be the one who gets hurt in the long run. Don't take the chance of ruining what could be a beautiful and compassionate relationship because of dishonesty or deceit.

8. Try to keep all commitments that you make.

Sometimes you will have to make personal sacrifices, but try to keep your commitments. If you find that you have to cancel appointments or make changes in your schedule let all people affected know ahead of time. Last minute changes are natural, normal and expected even though they are not always convenient. The most responsible person will have to make cancellations sometimes. It's life.

9. Set a good example by being a good example.

Deliver more than people expect from you. Giving more of yourself will help you to become more understanding. Don't get caught giving to others just to get something back. The idea of giving is to feel good about yourself and your good deeds, not to get more than you give.

10. Express confidence in your efforts.

As you go about your day, be sure to send positive rays of self-confidence. When talking, speak with energy and enthusiasm. The days you feel a little down and discouraged will have a positive effect on your state of being if you assert energy and spirit in what you do.

11. **Treat people as individuals.**

    Recognize each person has special skills or attributes that require a unique and different style of understanding. You are unique, beautiful and special, so is everyone you meet.

12. **Remain consistent.**

    If you are forgetful, and doubtful about the decisions you make, you will appear insecure. People will notice your insecurity or uneasiness and their trust and confidence in you will make them feel uncomfortable. Consistency reassures people of your trustworthiness.

13. **Don't allow discrimination to exist.**

    There is no room for discrimination in our world. Discrimination leads to problems and dangerous liaisons.

14. **To get ahead you must be well "informed."**

    Don't ever stop learning new things or seeking more information. Being informed will help you to become more knowledgeable and your conversation will have an added spark. People will love talking to you because you will have up to date information on many subjects and you'll know exactly what you're talking about.

15. Show people that you respect and trust them.

Don't express doubt about what a person tells you unless you are absolutely certain it is correct. Always treat it as an error before jumping to conclusions. Sometimes people will tell you things just to impress you; don't be angry with them for trying hard to be just like you. Acknowledge what they are saying and listen without judgment or benders.

16. Handle your problems efficiently.

Do not allow your problems to go unnoticed. Waiting on them to disappear will only cause you greater pain in the long run. Managing your problems in the beginning is the best way to avoid stress and make problems in the future.

17. Don't get so emotional that it gets the best of you.

Emotions are the reason people don't think logically. When you find your emotions taking over your life, first understand why you are allowing them to control you. Once you've figure out why list on a piece of paper the best way for you to handle them without causing disruptions in your life or the lives of others.

18. Do what you say you will do.

Living up to your promises will encourage people to support you. When your actions follow your words you don't have to work to impress people or try to win them over. In time, they see the strength of your character and line up to be on your support team.

19. Listen without judgment.

When you are a good listener people are devoted to you. Give the speaker your full attention. Don't interrupt, don't be distracted, and don't try to formulate your answers and thoughts while they are talking. Listen without judgment.

20. Pay what you owe when it is due.

Deferred payments and credit cards allowing you to buy now and pay later there is nothing that builds trust better than paying your debts promptly when due for services rendered.

21. Tell the truth about yourself and others.

To attract the trust of others always be truthful in regard to other people. If you are known to tell lies about other people, no one will want to associate with you? They will feel that you are deceitful and full of betrayal.

22. Be a source of strength.

If you want to have people whom you can lean on in troubled times you must provide a source of strength to them when they are in need. No one is strong all the time and even the weakest person has the power to provide support to those who trust and rely on them.

23. **Share without looking for praise or payment.**

    You can always tell who the do-good people are and who is there to simply look good. The do-good people do deeds without looking for rewards and on most occasions the rewards find you.

24. **Put the welfare of others before your own.**

    Be genuinely interested in seeing others succeed instead of promoting yourself all the time. In-kind actions show that you are as concerned about other people as you are about yourself.

A Moving Thought

We know that, when it comes to technology and the economy, if you're not constantly moving forward, then - without a doubt - you're moving backwards.

- Bill Owens

Chapter 12

Mindset 11: Reaching Goals Creatively

In this chapter you will learn the power of setting goals and develop a plan that will get you where you want to go.

Set Goals That Move You Forward

Your goals are the glue that keep you together. Once you understand the importance of setting goals you begin to set yourself firmly on the road to reaching them. Working daily to meet your goals will change your life drastically.

If you truly want to reach your desired level of success, you have to set specific goals. Your goals help you tap into your power source. Setting goals that are achievable, realistic and positive help you move in the right direction. Many times you have difficulty setting your goals because you don't know where to begin. Even though you know what you want when you want it, you probably still have difficulty going about getting it.

Have you ever had one of those days that you wake up on the wrong side of the bed, and you find yourself doing everything half-heartedly? Do you ever feel as if you are aimlessly drifting through life? Believe me; I know firsthand it doesn't feel good when you realize all the time you've wasted.

If you want to gain life's riches set realistic goals. If you don't; your hopes, dreams and beliefs will be short-lived. If you want to really change your life or do something completely different from the way you've always done it, you can't just sit around and wait on someone else to do it for you. You have to take the necessary steps to advance in a direction that's beneficial to you.

Sometimes We Fall

At the very beginning of my writing career I had it all; time money, success, cars, clothes, jewelry and multiple homes. I had received a seven figure contract that afforded me lifestyle of the rich and famous, but deep down inside I wasn't happy or satisfied. My family can tell you that I wasn't a nice person to be around. I was down-right mean. I had the money and lifestyle but things still weren't going smooth. The money didn't make all things fall in place. There were parts of my life that was still in chaos. My family didn't see the unhappiness that was in my heart and I was not in tune with life's true riches. I had to find a way to bring not only financial success to my life but also I had to find a way to bring balance in my overall life.

Does your life feel like it's off balance? The day to day grind can throw any hard working entrepreneur off balance. When you consider all the basic parts to becoming a success: manage meals, food, shelter, clothing, eating right, exercising, meetings, hobbies, work related activities, worshipping, and meaningful time to yourself, it can wear you out. Let's not forget your career so that you can have the money to take care of these parts of your lifestyle. When your family needs you to be there for love and support you have to be there for that too. It can take a toll on the most capable person. Physical wellbeing has to be at the top of our list, because if its not we cannot perform or function at our best. So are you ready to bring balance and order to your life? Are you ready to set some helpful long-term and short-term goals?

Setting Short-term and Long-term Goals

Short-term goals are those you reach in a minimum amount of time. Long-term goals get the job done in a specific time. Both inspire you to drive hard at attaining something you want. Maintaining balance with both short-term and long-term goals is a good way to accomplish your goals quicker.

When you set short-term goals you are looking for accomplishments sooner than later. Short-term goals give you a chance to trust yourself again. Goals are motivating forces that make you want to do better in life.

When you set goals and don't follow through, you have broken a promise to yourself, which is sometimes worse than breaking promises to others. You might think that what you say to your subconscious mind isn't really important, but it is. How often have you said you were going to do something that would help better your life and even though you knew it was good for you, you still didn't do it? Imagine the messages you've sent to your mind.

The best way to reach larger goals is to set smaller ones. When you set several small goals you're taking baby steps and taking baby steps help you reach bigger goals without feeling the pressures that accompany them.

Five Mindsets That Help You Set Goals and Win

1. Be honest.

As you work to build your life, you will add more value to what others think and feel about you. If they trust and believe in what you say and do they will respect you more. Trust is built on perceptions of honesty.

None of us are perfect at everything we do, and most of the time our intentions are good, but there will be times we won't be able to do everything we promised or said we would do. It's normal to make promises that we plan to keep but promises can be changed and affected by outside influences. If we are honest with people when we are not able to meet obligations or keep promises we maintain our credibility even when we fail.

2. Do the best work you can do.

What you put into any plan of action is reflected by how it turns out. Why waste your time doing something half-heartedly? If you do less, you achieve less, but if you do too much you can become unorganized and overwhelmed. A better understanding of how much you have to do will help you do the best work you can do.

3. Keep a positive outlook.

Get rid of the negative attitudes and negative thoughts. This includes negative relationships or anything that interferes with your ability to remain positive. You can't move forward if you're always thinking negative thoughts. You can't progress into a better relationship if you are involved in a negative relationship. The best way to gain power and receive better things in life is maintain a positive outlook and get rid of the negative influences in your life.

4. Think things through.

Do you have a wonderful capacity to think, but submit to the temptation to act before giving situations enough thought? So much of what we do is reaction because immediate action gives us gratification, but if we learn to think before we react we eliminate the possibility of numerous errors and crisis in our lives. People who think and plan out their lives benefit the most because their success rate is long-term.

5. Make a difference.

Your goals are definitely personal, but if you are trying to win in life and you don't include others you are doomed to fail. Find ways to help other people. When you operate from a helpful point of view others will want to be a part of your life and you will attract greater opportunities. You'll see opportunities where others see problems. You'll also see your problems as opportunities and won't allow others to talk you out of moving toward your success. You won't be afraid of challenges because you'll see them as stimulants to growth. Let's take a look at how you can give your goals power.

Giving Your Goals Power

- Your goals must be realistic.

  Your goals should be attainable and designed to build gradually so that your more difficult goals are set nearer to the end of the journey when you have built up confidence and determination through achieving the smaller ones.

- Your goals must be meaningful.

  Don't become limited in your goal setting. Your goals must be set with the possibility of leading you somewhere. If your goals are meaningful they become reachable.

  List three meaningful ways you can reach your goals?

  1. ______________________________
  2. ______________________________
  3. ______________________________

- Your goals must excite.

  Because your goals are your vision they must excite you. People around you may have good intentions and may have solid advice worth listening to, but you are the one who must make sure you reach your goals. Get excited about the things you need to do to reach the goals you set and then do what you need to reach them.

- **Your goals must be well defined.**

  Saying exactly what you want and mapping out a plan to get it will help you define your goals. Defining your goals is like making a wish list about how you are going to achieve the things you want. A well-defined action plan helps you reach goals.

- **Your goals require positive action.**

  Your goals should send you in the right direction. Setting goals and then acting upon them in order to achieve them not only moves you forward, it builds confidence in your ability to pursue them. Taking positive action helps you act on your dreams rather than just wishing or hoping for them.

- **Your goals must not isolate.**

  Of course it's terrifying when you're trying to reach your goals, but you should not shut yourself off from the world or the people you care about while reaching them. Getting all the things you wished, hoped and dreamed of having is great, but if you look around and there is no one there to share the glory it won't feel good, nor will it feel worthwhile.

- **Your goals must be written down.**

Written statements help us become more specific. Any and everything important to you should be committed in writing. Writing down a goal also helps internalize it. Look at your goals daily. The more specific your goals are - the better. Limit the statement to one or two sentences and make sure you understand what you wrote. A good mindset: 'If what you write won't fit on a 3 x 5 index card, it's too long.' If it takes the entire index card, you're not completely focused. Take time to think your goals through and condense them into short, understandable, action-oriented sentences.

- **Put your plan into action.**

Your goals give you a reason to take life on. When you have goals it shows that you have a plan and it manifests each day. All of your activities show that your goals are directed toward the actions necessary to reach them. Over time, develop projects that are directed toward future goals.

With a little planning you can do anything that you choose to do.

- **Create your personal timetable.**

  Your timetable should be precise, specific, and cut into bite-size pieces. Include activities to be completed and the time it's to be finished. Allow time for review or participation by everyone who might be affected by the outcome. Timetables help measure your success and are essential when you need to change your strategies or achievements.

- **Stay committed to your goals.**

  Changing your life requires sticking to your commitment until it becomes a mindset. Keeping your eyes on your target helps you reach your goals. Obstacles are those frightening things you see when you take your eyes off the target. Remember when you are trying to reach your goals - anything and everything that can go wrong - will go wrong. Stick with the plan and all will work out just fine.

A Moving Thought

If everyone is moving forward together,
then success takes care of itself.

- Henry Ford

Chapter 13

Mindset 12: Building Your Success Ladder

In this chapter you will learn how to create your own ladder of success so that you can bring balance to all areas of your life.

Enjoying Big and Small Successes

Dreams do come true! Whenever your life is foggy your dreams become distant, but on the flip side dreams can be like automobile headlights, illuminating your paths, making it easier for you to get where you are trying to go. As you create your ladder of success you learn to dream. As you dream it's easier to take the steps needed to get where you want to go.

You cannot do much about outside forces such as things people say about you or the perceptions they have of you. You would do better to focus on those successful things that are within your control. I liked to refer to those things as your ladder of success. For the purpose of this book, let's consider a ladder of success with three rings on it labeled career, relationships and community. These are primary areas that create a better life and generate success for you.

Your first ring is your relationship ring. It might include your family, spouse, partner or friends. This is perhaps the most important area because it affects all other areas of your life. Without strong relationships it's difficult to build a meaningful life. A person may have career and community success, but without friends, family and loved ones, these things may not be enough. A life without strong mutually supportive relationships can be a hollow existence.

Your second ring is your career. Having a wonderful job or career is highly important in building a better life. You need something to give your life structure and your career provides that.

The third ring is your community, which might include your neighborhood, city, church, school district, county and state. Your role may involve volunteer work holding an appointed or elected office working on a neighborhood committee or participation and involvement in your church. This category includes any role outside the home or office that involves you in the lives of other people and the world around you. By getting involved with your community you will discover greater opportunities.

	Career	Relationships	Community
1.			
2.			
3.			
4.			
5.			
6.			
7.			
8.			
9.			
10.			

To help understand how important your ladder of success is, here's what you can do: Make a list of the three categories. Within each make a list of ten things you can do to get rid of any unwanted or bad mindsets. Making changes or improvements in your personal life - relationships, job or career, or your place in the community can help you replace bad mindsets with new and better mindsets.

Some of the categories you listed might have the same improvements. They might include spending more time with someone you love and doing the things that both of you enjoy, such as getting more education or helping others improve their lives in some way.

Your ladder of success is designed to help you focus on what you really want in life, but it doesn't have to be limited to three categories. You could come up with a dozen or more categories, but for now let's focus on these three because they are the three key elements of your lives. If things are not going well in these areas of your life chances are they will have a negative impact on other areas of your life. They all affect one another in some way or another, which is perfectly normal. That's why it's important to have a balanced life. With a balanced life you are able to pay attention to your relationships, your job, career, and community around you whether that means your neighbors, your city, church, or the region in which you live.

You might develop a more specific ladder of success later, one that will include other interests in your life. What would you say your ladder of success consist of today?

Your Ladder Can Overlap Sometimes

Note that your ladder of success will sometimes overlap, which is perfectly normal. An example of these overlapping areas is relationships and community, which may also include friends who are co-workers, and your best friend who might also live in the same apartment complex you live in. Maybe even next door to you. This type of overlapping can be overlapped even more if your best friend is dating a family member. If your job is full time parenting, your relationship and job duties will overlap a great deal. If you are a public servant, then sometimes your career and your community ladder of success will overlap.

I believe these key areas of your life will strengthen your quality of life. It will give you a more solid base from which to achieve a better life. Designing your own ladder of success will help your dreams materialize. *It is the responsibility of people to design their own ladder of success.* The importance of having your own ladder of success will make you feel more dedicated to climbing it if you want it for yourself.

There Are Plans for Your Success

Sometimes, when we experience failure we believe that God does not always want us to experience success or financial gain. The truth is … God is interested in all we do that helps us succeed. He is interested in the smallest details of our lives. He wants us to succeed and be happy. God wants to bless each and every one of us. We should not expect our entire blessing to be financial either. Blessings come in many forms. God gives us the desires in our heart (Psalm 37:4).

We are supposed to enjoy God, communicate with Him and live our lives as an extension of His love. In other words when we connect with God, He will plant the seed of His divine purpose, desires, and aspirations in our hearts and then bring them into existence. God is honest, so you can believe in Him.

Climbing Your Ladder of Success

Look around; you can see people who are climbing their ladder of success. They range from athletes, to civic and civil rights leaders, preachers, friends, neighbors, your children and even business partners. You can see the success ladder in the lives of your closest family members too. Your ladder is designed to help you become a more positive person for yourself and others.

The steps described here are not miracle cures or magical, they are merely active steps that will help you find happiness and success in life. They will help you improve yourself; whether you are entering the workplace out of high school or college, looking to start your own business, entering into the corporate world or just starting over into a new relationship or career.

As you follow these steps, you'll learn a lot about yourself. You'll discover the biggest obstacles blocking your road to happiness are those things that you unconsciously put in your own path: past hurts, negative attitudes, poor self-image and the notion that you are a victim of life rather than a wonderful life force. The following steps can free you to pursue your visions.

Successful Things You Can Do

Successful people do whatever it takes to get them where they want to be. The key to your success is not what you do…it's how you feel about what you are doing. It's very possible to take basic ideas and create higher levels of success. Success begins with an asset that is worth more than money. It begins with a positive attitude. Your successes are not bought or inherited they are within. They begin with you!

What is the key to gaining higher levels of success? The sick will say health; the poor will guess wealth; the ambitious believe it is power and influence; and the intellectual will say knowledge. Few people realize that success in life depends more upon what they *are* than upon what they *know*. It is confidence that has brought us this far. All high achieving people recognize that attitude is everything. High achievers shoot for the stars and if they fail, they never stay down, they learn from their adversity. If they fall down five times they get up six times. Are you willing to get up more times than you fall? Circle one: Yes ____ or No_____?

You Are Worthy of Success

The road to success is a worthy one to take. Successful people take chances and they walk to the beat of a different drummer. High achievers come early and stay late; they make a forty-hour workweek look like child's play. Those who are committed to personal excellence dream big dreams and they work hard to make those dreams come true. Ultimately, high achievers make choices instead of excuses; they know that any excuse is a reason for inactivity. Most important they know that they are responsible for the outcome of their success. The following checklist is great for people looking to improve their climb toward success.

- ### Associate with people who think and act positive.

  If the people around you are not motivated or stumbling toward an uncertain future it will adversely affect you and your performance. It's important that you spend lots of time with those who are optimistic and motivated.

- ### Follow the mindsets of motivation.

  (a) Get started. (b) Keep working toward your goal. Put one foot in front of the other. (c) Keep your eyes open, and see each goal through until they are completed.

- **Learn from your mistakes.**

  All things of value, great or small, were created from gathered wisdom. To achieve the wisdom that you desire you should have experiences. Mistakes are useful experiences when you learn from them. Have an attitude of learning from everything that you do and you will win.

- **Give yourself time to complete your goals.**

  By adding an extra week or month to the date to reach a certain goal, you erase false hopes. Wake up an hour early for no reason at all or go to bed an hour later. Use the extra hour to list your daily, weekly or even your monthly goals.

- **Make small, positive decisions regularly.**

  Make decisions every day to do those small things that you sometimes overlook.

- **Take small steps toward reaching your goals.**

  Dare to accomplish your goals by taking the small steps toward reaching them. Break large tasks into smaller, less stressful ones. Think of your tasks as smaller pieces instead of one large task. Work on one piece at a time and they it's easier to handle over a period of time.

- **Think of your successes during your task.**

  Think about how well you did it and the steps you took to remain motivated. Embellish how you felt when you completed your task successfully. Feel the emotion and excitement of that same energy over to your present task.

- **Wear a T-shirt with motivating messages on it.**

  This is an inexpensive way to bring inspiration and motivation to your life, and its well worth it.

- **Analyze things that make goals difficult to reach.**

  Find out which negative factors are obvious? Handle these obstacles early on to avoid problems later on. This will help your chances of success improve.

- **Always have an alternate plan of action.**

  Even when you know for sure that you will succeed you still need to have an alternate plan. What will you do if things don't happen the way you planned them to? With an alternate plan you will have less stress and more options.

- **Take a mind break every hour or so.**

  The brain needs a moment to rest sometimes, so get up and stretch. Take in some slow deep breaths, climb some stairs, go for a walk, a jog, or a bike ride. Relax your mind, body and spirit often.

- **Set goals that will motivate and inspire you.**

  Make goals believable and exciting so that they challenge you without discouraging you. Set goals for health, vitality and improving relationships. When you have powerful goals your motivation becomes ignited.

- **Have heart-to-heart talks with your elders.**

  Make sure you talk to someone over 60 years of age. Ask what motivating forces helped them reach their goals. Senior citizens have oodles of wisdom. The information they provide can help you to remain focused.

- **Make sure your tasks have positive values.**

  Realize that personal accomplishments will make you feel good. Associate your goals with making yourself a richer or better. Think of what you do as gaining inspiration.

- **Remain conservative when things go wrong.**

  Brainstorm on how you can reduce the risks in your life. Analyze what you can prevent and then proceed with confidence to achieve what you desire.

- **Know that change is necessary to succeed.**

  Knowing that it's okay to change is healthy and rewarding. Even unwanted change can help you succeed.

- **Take passion walks from time to time.**

  As you take your walk, think of the most passionate goals that you want to accomplish. Let your passion inspire you to reach higher to achieve your goals.

- **Believe in yourself with conviction.**

  Reaching your goals will be greater if you surround yourself with a positive support system. Believing in yourself is a key feature in reaching your goals.

- **Keep souvenirs of successes.**

  Little reminders scattered about your home or office will keep you motivated and encouraged.

- **Don't ever stop learning.**

  Engage your brain in the process of learning. Challenge your mind's capabilities to learn new things and you will.

- **Remain flexible.**

  Be able to handle change and also be prepared to change at a moment's notice.

- **Have a special place you can go and think.**

  On top of your favorite mountain, in your car, on a bike ride, in a hot tub, or by your favorite window. Make sure it's a place you feel inspired, motivated and encouraged.

- **Get excited about the small things in life.**

  Allow your smallest joys to bring excitement into your life. Get hyped on life and celebrate small victories.

- **Meet with people who have common interest.**

  Meet to report each other's progress and exchange ideas that will help motivate one another. Name your group something motivational also. Take turns meeting at each other's homes or at different places to bring encouragement and motivation.

- **Let your down times motivate you.**

  Let your bad times motivate you to do better or achieve more so that bad won't happen again. Let feeling bad inspire you to achieve your goals.

- **Eliminate expectations that will not happen.**

  Accept and enjoy what does happen. Believe and accept that what happens to and for you will help you to achieve the things that you want to achieve.

- **Become ruthlessly honest with yourself.**

  Ask yourself questions so that you can congratulate yourself after answering them. Be your own best friend.

- **Program yourself to think success.**

  Each time you have a moment of free time, think of your goals. Silently talk to yourself. Before you fall asleep repeat your goals to yourself. It's like counting sheep except you'll recite your goals in the place of sheep. Think about achieving them, picture yourself achieving them, and make them real in your imagination.

- **Create verbal and written contract with yourself.**

  Identify your goals or tasks. Write them down; record the date you want to complete these things and how you want to go about reaching them.

- **Focus on your self-concept.**

  Know that you're already motivated. If you make the

choices that are good for your career and future, your actions will demonstrate your motivational skills. Now transfer some of that energy to the other tasks that you aren't quite as motivated about.

- **Stay in best physical shape that you can.**

  Having a physically fit body gives you the vim, vigor and vitality to accomplish your goals. When you have physical energy you have mental energy.

- **Don't live in the past.**

  If you find yourself living in the past think of something that you have to be thankful for. You are free to do other things so be thankful for that also. Now move forward.

- **Change the times that you do your tasks.**

  Since motivation levels change throughout the day, you should vary the time of the day that you fulfill obligations. Energy levels are different at different times of the day. Your productivity will definitely increase as a result of your variations.

- **Keep inspirational photos visible.**

  Post photos of people, places and things that motivate you in a very visual place. This will keep you motivated.

- **Bribe yourself with your favorite rewards.**

  When you reach your goals, reward yourself so that you will be able to celebrate your successes. It's fun and encouraging to receive rewards and feel successful?

- **Learn to reach your goals without griping.**

  Meet the world head on. Understand your happiness and willingness to move forward without griping. With all the chaos, complexity and turmoil you've got to learn to deal with life's ups and downs. Rise above petty complaints and embrace the joys of the world.

- **Visualize your successes.**

  Talk to God and give thanks for each and every blessing you receive. Visualize your life and be thankful what for you have. Give thanks and then be thankful.

- **Decide what your goals, dreams, and visions are.**

  Work every day toward achieving them. Whatever inspires you should also motivate you.

- **Take thirty minutes of quiet time each day.**

  The best time to indulge in quiet time is when your life seems to be moving too fast or filled with problems.

Acknowledge your goals and dreams while meditating. Then plan a better way to achieve your goals.

- **Use motivating language on a daily basis.**

  Incorporate it into your vocabulary. Your attitude will become positive if you use positive words more often.

- **Create your own motivational tape.**

  Listen to it each day upon waking. Record your goals, dreams, aspirations and those things that help keep you motivated. Give yourself a pep talk every day. You can add music to your tape if you like.

- **Create a road map to your success.**

  Create signs and markers on a make shift road map that will help lead you in the right direction. Include anything that you feel will be beneficial to your success. If you should get lost or lose focus, pull out your road map and study it from time to time to gain focus again. Follow your road map each day until you reach your goals.

Success is often the result of taking a misstep in the right direction.

\- Al Bernstein

A Moving Thought

I cannot say whether things will get better if we change;
what I can say is that they must change if they are to get better.

Chapter 14

Mindset 13: Appreciating Spiritual Power

In this chapter you learn to draw upon sources that inspire you to get closer to the truths of all humanity – your spiritual power.

Drawing Upon Your Power

Two couples were sitting at their normal meeting place. It was a cozy restaurant on the north side of Dallas, Texas. They had arranged this dinner to get out of the house for a while and try to have some fun. While talking about how things had been going in their lives their discussion drifted into a discussion of personal difficulties and problems. One man was especially despondent. Then, his girlfriend and friends, realized his unhappy state of mind and noticed how concerned he was with his problems. They hoped a few hours sharing time with close friends would get his mind off his problems.

As the couple sat trying to come up with some type of positive solution they offered various suggestions to him. Finally the happier couple decided to call it a night. They had also experienced difficulties from time to time. Another man who was about to leave, looked at the despondent man and placed his hand on the man's shoulder and said "I hope you won't think I'm preaching to you, because I'm not, but I'd like to offer you a word of advice: "Why not draw upon on your spiritual power?"

He shook his friends hand affectionately and left the group. The despondent man sat thinking about this. Finally, he looked at his girlfriend and said, "Honey, I know what he means and I know what my spiritual power is. I only wish I knew how to draw upon it. It's what I need right now." He knew that the advice he received at the restaurant was solid and very wise.

There are many people today who are unhappy and depressed and not getting anywhere with themselves or with their problems. And they do not want it to be that way - really they don't.

It took a while for the despondent man, but after long hours and thinking and mediation he has finally learned how to draw upon his spiritual power and it has changed everything for him. Now he's a healthier and happier man. If only he had known the secrets to draw from his spiritual power sooner than later. Maybe you are having problems and you need a better understanding of how to draw upon your spiritual power. If you are here are several things you can do:

- First, learn to read and understand your bible.
- Second, gain a relationship with God by communicating to him on a regular basis.
- Third, learn from what you read and incorporate things that with help you move forward in your life.
- Fourth, practice depending upon God and pray for support and power.
- Fifth, rest assured that God hears your prayers.
- Sixth, believe that God is giving it to you and stay in touch with that power.

There are ways to draw upon your spiritual power.

Let Your Prayers Flow

Yield yourself to prayer, let it flow through and do it in a relaxed and confident manner. Those who wait upon the Lord shall be renewed in personal and spiritual strength. Even though your life can become filled with many things to do, if you use prayer as your power you will have all the spiritual strength you need.

Take Optimistic Attitudes toward Every Problem

The amount of faith that you must bring forth will help you receive the power you need to handle your difficult situations. "According to your faith be it unto you," (Matthew 9:29) is a basic law of spiritual living.

Spiritual power can do wonders for you. Draw upon it and experience its great benefits and helpfulness. Why remain defeated when all you have to do is draw upon your spiritual power. To take optimistic attitudes toward your problems…

- State your problem and ask for a specific answer.
- Believe that you will receive the answer.
- Believe that through God's help you are constantly gaining power over your difficult situations.

When your faith is renewed your healing power and trust is complete. spiritual power is one of the most amazing facets in human existence. I am awestruck at the thorough-going, tremendous, overwhelming changes for the good it accomplishes in the lives of people.

It's so easy for me to recite story after story that I am familiar with, but I do this because I know that the people who experienced this kind of power have had a new birth of life.

If You Ever Feel Lost Simply Pray

Your spiritual power is constantly available to you and if you ever feel lost simply pray. If you open your mind, heart and soul to prayer it will rush in to you like a wonderful burst of energy. It is there for anybody who lives under any circumstances or in any condition. This wonderful inflow of power moves you in a direction with such force that in the rush it drives everything before it; casting out fear, hate, sickness, weakness, moral defeat, scattering them as though they had never touched you, refreshing and restraining your life with health, happiness and goodness.

Why Draw Upon Your Spiritual Power?

Having the will to depend upon your spiritual power comes from your inner strength. The working of this power in your life is the most moving and thrilling manifestation of power of any kind.

No matter what your problems are, the fact that your spiritual power can heal most any difficulty and problem in your life emphasizes the tremendous truth related in this chapter and throughout this book.

Almost all problems, difficulties, or defeats can be solved or overcome by faith, positive thinking, and prayer to God. The good thing is that the techniques are simple and workable. Why not draw upon your spiritual power? It works! “To achieve great things in life - live as though you're never going to fail.”

Learn to Pray Effectively

If you choose prayer as your means of communicating; the best way to begin is to first form a constant relationship with God. Because prayer is somewhat personal the relationship you have with God will also be constant and personal.

Prayer and its effectiveness is based upon the relationship one has with God. There are prayers in the bible that Jesus prayed that can be studied to improve your prayer techniques. One's relationship with God affects the way they pray. Prayer is a great and powerful form of communication.

Answer these questions:

1. How strong is your relationship with God?

2. How strong is your communication with God?

Renewing Your Spiritual Power

Renewing your spiritual power provides leadership in your life. It’s highly related to your personal leadership skills. Spiritual power is your center and commitment to your value system. It’s a very personal area of life, yet it can be used publicly, and is very important to living a successful life. It draws upon the sources that inspire, lift and motivate us to timeless truths of all humanity.

You can find personal renewal in your daily prayers by meditating and reciting scriptures. You'll find strength in dealing with people more effectively because they represent your value system. As you read and meditate you'll began to feel renewed, strengthened, recommitted and centered to serve.

Are You Just a Little Depressed?

I'd like to share an intimate story of my own spiritual renewal with you. This is a little story I call, "I'm Just A Little Depressed." It tells of a time when I was feeling everything and everybody was unbalanced in my life. My enthusiasm was at an all-time low; my teaching efforts were fruitless; and my writing efforts were lacking. My personal situation was growing worst by the day.

Finally, I was determined to seek professional help from a medical doctor. Observing that I had nothing physically wrong with me the doctor asked if I could follow his instruction for at least one full day.

When I assured him that I could, he told me to spend the following day in a place where I could feel my happiest. My instructions were as follows: I could take food and drinks with me, but I was not to talk to anyone, read, write, listen to the radio or watch television. He then handed me four prescriptions he had written as we were talking. He numbered them and then he instructed me to open one at ten, twelve, two and four o'clock.

After looking over his prescriptions, I looked at him and then asked, "Are you serious?"

He said, "You won't think I'm joking once you start taking these prescriptions!"

The First Prescription: 10:00 AM

The next day I went to the vacant lot where I had envisioned my dream house would be built someday. I sat there gazing into space for about ten minutes, and then I opened the first prescription.

It read, *"Close your eyes and listen carefully for the next two hours."*

I thought my doctor had lost his mind. How could I sit still long enough to listen with my eyes closed for two hours? But, since I had agreed to follow instructions, I closed my eyes and listened. The first sounds I heard were lots of birds chirping and the wind whistling through the trees. I could also hear motorboats and water noise. After about fifteen minutes I could hear other noises that I hadn't noticed at first. As I listened, my body began to relax. I found myself seeking to listen for more wonderful sounds.

I began to hear the wind blowing against my face, the trees swaying in the wind and suddenly I felt patience, respect and renewed awareness of the joy of being alive. I began to listen to the sounds - the silence - the peacefulness and then suddenly I began to feel very calm and at peace with who I am. I laid there feeling peace within.

The Second Prescription 12:00 Noon

At noon, I opened the second prescription and read it. It read, *"Recall pleasant moments by going back into times when your life was happier."*

I thought, "When was the last time I was truly happy?" It took me a while to recall happier times, but as I closed my eyes and meditated about it I found that the last time I was truly and honestly happy was when I was in college. No bills, worries or major responsibilities to bring me down. It was the most carefree time of my life. My moments of joy and success were clearer now. I could feel a warm and tingly feeling on my insides. I could also feel myself smiling at the thought of these moments. I laughed out loud at the memories of the good ole days.

The Third Prescription: 2:00 PM

At two o'clock, I read the third prescription. Until now these prescription were pretty easy to take, but this one was different. It read, *"What Are Your Motives?"*

At first I was a little confused and defensive. I thought what do my motives have to do with this? Then I remembered my promise I made to my doctor and thought about what my motives were. I wanted success, recognition and financial security and I justified them all. The thought occurred to me that these motives weren't good enough, so I thought about it a little longer. Suddenly the answer came to me, my motives were not right and that's why everything had appeared to be so wrong to me. That's why I had been moving in the wrong direction – a direction that was not helping me live my dreams or really reach my most desired goals. I began to understand why it was taking me so long to find happiness and peace of mind. My motives were not in sync with what God wanted me to do.

It makes no difference what you are doing in life - whatever it is - as long as you are serving only yourself you won't succeed for very long. When you are serving others; happiness comes in abundance. It creates a gravitational experience. When you are selfish it pulls you down and you find yourself constantly spiraling in a downward spiral. The law of gravity cannot be defied when you fail to help others.

Now, I know that my motives for success have to be alignment with what's right for not only me, but others too.

The Fourth Prescription: 4:00 PM

When four o'clock came, I opened the fourth and final prescription. This one was easy to fill. It said, *"State Your Worries Aloud."* I thought for a few minutes then recited my worries aloud. It was as if I had released my worries into the universe for a helping hand. Afterwards I stood up, stared into the sky and then I headed home.

Your Experience Can Be Peaceful

I thought about the activities of this day as I drove home. It was a peaceful and beautiful experience for me. It was also richly rewarding. These exercises caused me to stop and think about what is right and best for me during tough times. I often do these same exercises when my schedule is hectic and I haven't had a chance to take a breather. It does wonders for getting me in tune with the world around me and the gifts of life. I can honestly say that at this moment it was an experience of peace and fulfillment.

Experience Spiritual Renewal?

Reading great literature, listening to great music and enjoying life can provide a renewal of the spirit for some. There are others who find it in the way they communicate with nature. Nature places blessings on those who immerse themselves in it. When you're able to leave the noise and discord of the city and give yourself the harmony and the rhythm of nature, you will experience renewal.

Spiritual renewal offers an investment of time. It's an activity that you should not neglect. You've probably heard the great Martin Luther King Jr. say, "I've got so much to do today I'll have to spend another hour on my knees." To him prayer was not a mechanical duty, but a source of power in releasing and multiplying energies.

The idea is that when you take time to draw on your spiritual power you also learn what life is ultimately all about and it spreads like an umbrella over everything else. It renews, protects, refreshes, and even more so - it reconfirms your faith if you recommit to it.

Create Your Own Spiritual Mission Statement

A spiritual mission statement is important in everybody's life. You write a mission statement for the purpose of achieving goals.

You see mission statements at work, but how often have you written your very own spiritual mission statement. Do this today!

If you write it down you are more likely to commit to it and have an understanding of your life's purpose. When you write it down you can review and recommit to it. In your daily renewal, you can visualize and "live out" the events of the day in harmony with values intact.

Battles of Your Soul Can Be Settled

The greatest battles of life are fought out daily in the silent chambers of your soul. If you can win battles here, if you can settle the issues that inwardly conflict with your beliefs, you'll feel a sense of peace - a sense of knowing what you're about.

It is here - in your soul - where you'll think cooperatively to promote the welfare of yourself and good of other people and to be genuinely happy for others and their successes. It is here that by drawing upon your spiritual power your own successes will flow naturally. Make peace with your soul and you win the battle with your spiritual self.

God is opening doors for great opportunities that you can use when its time to share your gifts. When you share and give to others so that you can help them succeed and become better at who they are God rewards you abundantly. When you are happy and love what you are doing you don't mind helping others gain insight. You don't mind offering your time and services to mentor someone coming up in the ranks behind you.

And in the end it's not the years in your life that count.
It's the life in your years.
- Abraham Lincoln

Chapter 15

Mindset 14: Enhancing Your Life Purpose

In this chapter you will learn why it's important to have purpose. Once you discover your purpose you thirst for a successful life.

What Is Your Purpose?

It was a day just like any other day when the principal of the inner city school I was working summoned me to his office. I was preparing my senior students for their final exam, but I was getting all kinds of interruptions.

First and most important I couldn't find my roll book; second, one of my students, who was a popular athlete had been cutting classes every day. Third, grades were almost due to the registrar's office so students were under pressure.

There was one female student who expected to pass the course even though she had attended class only three times for the entire semester. I had already contacted her mother weeks before, but she never responded to my failure report notices. So; naturally, I would have to tell her that her daughter wasn't going to graduate.

Our principal was the kind of guy who showed favor to athletes so he allowed many good teachers to be walked on by parents. I was in the mindset of covering my butt in every sense of the way. I recognized that my boss was a guy that was easily manipulated long before I began to have problems with some of the parents.

Every parents has moments when they think they're child can do no wrong. I have caught myself in the same situation with my daughter. She would get into trouble and then come back with a pitiful story to make me think it was the teacher's fault. But, because I had been teaching more than twenty-five years I was not easily convinced of her innocence.

Anyway, when my principal called me into the office he asked me what was going on with one of my students named Nick. I explained to him that she had forty-five unexcused absences and would possibly not graduate with her class. He asked was there anything else I could do, I told him she could turn in all of her incomplete assignments, but by law she had not been in class the state required amount of days.

He sat there motionless for about five minutes and then said to me; "I'm going to have to put you on administrative leave of absence until I investigate this matter." I was stunned at his decision to take such unorthodox action.

"What investigation I thought?" All he had to do was check the data on her and see that she had been absent for more than the required days as a senior student to qualify for graduation. Without anything further said he asked me to leave the campus. I was frozen in time, I could not believe this was happening.

I gave him the hardest look I could give him and then I went back to my classroom to pack my things. Another teacher helped me take my things to my car. The following days were torture for me because I loved my job. Teaching was my dream job. It didn't pay much, but I wasn't in it for the money.

I didn't sleep at all that night, but I struggled through it. The first thing I did on the next day was contact a lawyer and tried to make legal sense of everything. After meeting with my lawyer we felt that I had good case. I began to deal with what was happening to me. Some days were better than others though.

Getting Through Difficult Times

I mentioned keeping a journal in Chapter 5, but I recall when I began my purposeful journaling. I had been laid off work. This was the first time in my life since I began to work that I had ever been off work. To help me deal with my discomfort I started journaling. I recorded everything that was important in my life. Every time I felt bad I wrote it down. Every time I wanted to cry I wrote it down. I wrote why I was feeling the way I felt. Believe me my positive journal helped me get through my most difficult times.

Two years later I still had not heard anything from my principal or the School District. I was getting paid to sit at home and do nothing. I was paid my normal salary every month for three years without incident. I didn't understand it, but I kept quiet. I was getting paid more money to stay at home than to go to work each day. Not a bad set-up I thought. I thought to myself God works in mysterious ways.

Come To Your Senses

When I finally came to my senses and decided I would not feel sorry for myself, I decided that I had to get past my turmoil. I had lost my job a few weeks earlier and I was sulking. This was my door into finding my purpose.

I would come into the pleasure of writing my first book. While on my leave of absence from work I became involved with women shelters that needed volunteers. I began to research how I could assist these women even more. I visited malls, expos and movie theaters so that I could find groups of people who would freely express their views about women's issues. I kept busy and at the same time it helped me find my true purpose in life.

Today, instead of in small classroom settings I am now teaching worldwide. Now, I don't feel as though others are controlling my life.

After being fired I have now taken my life back and I am in control of my destiny. I have found a way to fulfill my purpose by writing books that can help women in more ways than one. Why don't you take this time to think for a few minutes and really discover what your purpose is? Really think about it in depth. Discover the 'who' you want to be and then get moving in a direction that will help you find your true purpose.

Finding Your True Purpose

Many of us live from day to day without a real sense of purpose. We know that we want more out of life, but we can't seem to put a finger on exactly what it is. We believe our fate is due to a lack of something - career, money, material possessions, spirituality or the freedom to do what we want.

Actually, what you may be longing for is your true life's purpose. When you have a mission you wholeheartedly embrace your tasks and you remain focused until your tasks are done. When you have a purpose you feel valued, worthy and respectable. You manage to keep your spirit up because you are living for you.

Our life's purpose has often been compared to an athletic game, and this analogy is useful when trying to find your primary purpose in life. By learning what your purpose in life, you can also discover what your true destiny is.

Now is Your Time

By now you know that you deserve the best things in life, but more and more people are discovering that in order to get the things they desire and deserve in life they have to find their purpose. Finding your purpose isn't as difficult as you might think. It can be fun. There is no more valuable step than to ask one question, "What is my individual role in the Universe?"

Once you learn the answer to this question you benefit fully from the beauty, power and perfection of your wonderful universe. Your awareness of your purpose develops your sense of belonging. It allows you to see yourself as an essential part of a much larger experience and you no longer feel separate or alone.

When you are truly aware of your purpose, whatever obstacles occur appears meaningful. No longer will you see situations as isolated. You will see them as significant events in your life. Furthermore, there is no way that goodness and abundance or success can come to you if you are not living with a purpose in life. The universe is an orderly system of activities and events. Things flow in and out and through. Think of your purpose in life as giving to God and know that God will give back to you. You must be willing to live with a purpose if you really want to fuel your passion.

Ignite Your Engine

While igniting your engine is next to the final step it by no means is the least important step. Moving in the right direction aides you in making the total commitment to your life-long vision for a better life and you go all-out in pursuit of it.

This means never losing focus so that you will keep the desire to achieve more in your life. It doesn't matter whether it's your job, career, family, friends or the role you play in your community. By making the commitment to find your purpose and have a better life you open doors that would otherwise remain closed.

Succeed In Spite of What Others Think

Most of us think we can do all things until someone tells us we cannot do it. We are willing to try anything, go anywhere stretch ourselves to the limit in pursuit of our dreams and then we talk to other people and they remind us of how dangerous it could be, how ridiculous it sounds and what a chance we are taking.

People have no problem informing us of all the downsides and pitfalls. They cannot see how we will ever reach our goal. They put us in touch with our faults; remind us of our mistakes, limitations and mindsets. They remind us of all the others who tried and didn't make it, and in vivid detail they tell us why we can't do this or that. They give us warnings, cautions and helpful hints about alternative things we can do. When they are finished we have been effectively talked out of our dreams. We have lost our belief in ourselves.

Take Your Leap of Faith

If you have a dream and you are committed to it the only way to it is through it. You must take the chance and the leap of faith. If you believe in yourself and in your ability your commitment will help you soar.

A Moving Thought

When faced with a decision – decide.
When faced with a choice – choose.
When you don't do anything you neither win nor lose.

Chapter 16

Mindset 15:

Incorporating Affirmations

In this chapter you receive examples of affirmations, reminders and visualizations and how to apply them to most any situation.

Visualizations, Self-talk, and Reminders

A**s you think, so shall you be.** It's best to flush out tired, outdated, and worn-out thoughts and fill your mind with fresh, new, creative thoughts of faith, love, and goodness. Affirmations can actually remake your life.

I know many people who are modest, but they never let anything get them down. Problems, setbacks, nor opposition cannot get them down. They simply attack their difficulties with an optimistic attitude and the sure confidence that it will work out right. And it always does for them. They seem to have a magic way of life - a way that never fails. You probably know at least one person like that too.

Because of these impressive characteristics some of these people have caught my attention. I knew that there was an explanation for them being able to do everything just right. I wanted to hear their story and learn how I could use what they do to make my life and others fall into place. It's not easy to persuade people to talk about themselves.

Repeat Positive Statements Intently

Our positive statements are our affirmations, self-talk, reminders, & visualizations. They are our sentences or positive statements repeated with the intention of convincing us they are true. They are best used when written down or posted in places where we can see them, and say them aloud. There is nothing mysterious about affirmations, self-talk, reminders or visualizations. They work on sound psychological principles that will help change and improve your life. I have listed many affirmations throughout this book- at the beginning and end of each chapter to help you get an idea of how they work.

Affirmations aren't new, but they sure are making a comeback. Many people use them and have for many years. If you think about it, you will also realize that you use them consciously and unconsciously. They are the steady streams of noise that goes on in your head. Everyone has these mental conversations from time to time. It's called self-talk or mind-talk.

Unfortunately, many times what you tell yourself is negative. You can say things that will make you feel insecure or unsure such as: "I can't do this," "I'm dumb," "I never do anything right," "I'm the worst person to be alive." If you continue to talk negatively to yourself you will soon began to believe the things you say.

Reverse Any Negative Self-Talk

You can learn to reverse your negative way of thinking. Use affirmations to help you learn the positive truths about yourself. You can learn to substitute destructive self-talk for constructive self-talk.

Choose to use affirmations that are the most beneficial and helpful to you. Find a special place that's quiet so you can say them aloud to yourself. Do this several times a day until they are a natural part of your daily life. Repeat one affirmation at least five times each day and by the end of the week your affirmations should be firmly embedded in your memory and you should be able to recall them whenever you need them.

Everyone else will have his or her own way of using self-talk. Your self-talk may sometimes be at odds with what other people expect of you because people usually want to benefit from how you act and react.

Two Kinds of Beliefs

Affirmations work because they narrow the gap between two kinds of beliefs. One belief holds what you absolutely know is a fact, such as your birth date, your name or the color of your eyes. The other beliefs are those that you intellectually accept, but maybe you haven't put them into practice yet, such as, believing that you are unique and different and that alone makes you a good person.

Once you began to believe your affirmations they actually help you overcome personal obstacles that keep you from loving yourself. At first these ideas will be a part of your walking consciousness, but in time they become a permanent parts of your belief system. Once the new belief is accepted it is accepted as true. It then has an immediate impact on your life. The more you think about it being true, the greater its effect on you. As you repeat your affirmations, they continually remind you of situations or conditions you wish to create. The more you think about them, the more real they become.

Create Your Own Affirmations

You can find affirmations just about anywhere you look, from bumper stickers on cars to billboards, TV commercials, beauty salons, malls, airports, books, and clothing stores. Some will even seem to be calling your name when you read them. School districts, large companies, athletic teams and churches use affirmations regularly. If you want to create your own, here are some things that you should remember:

1. Try not to use negatives or derogatory terms and phrases in affirmations. Keep affirmations positive and life enhancing.

2. Try to keep affirmations short and snappy. Short affirmations help you remember them. You are likely, to use them more if you can remember them.

3. Don't use others behavior in affirmations. Your affirmations should say things that reflect a change or improvement in your life. If you include others, it will frustrate you. Remember the focus here is to improve through positive thinking.

4. Keep affirmations in the present tense. Instead of saying things in the past like, "I should have done better on my test," or the future "I will do better on my final," say, "I did better today and

that will help me in the future." By using affirmations in the future tense you might postpone them indefinitely.

5. Self-talk and daily affirmations such as those in this book are one way to remind you of your strengths. Combining several of them and saying them aloud is a great way to gain personal strength in your daily life.

Knowing When to Use Affirmations

One of the best times to use affirmations is when you are putting yourself down. They help counter attack negative self-statements with positive self-statements. They also eliminate the negative effects of your past.

One of my closest friends, named Marie has a bad habit of putting herself down. She even found ways to help others put her down. Marie dated a man named Melvin. After losing her teaching job Melvin convinced Marie that they should be married after only two months of dating. The "put downs" started soon after Marie said "I Do."

On the day of their wedding, they argued from the moment they got on the plane in the United States all the way to the Caribbean Islands. It got so bad Melvin refused to consummate their marriage on their honeymoon.

After about four months of marriage Valentine's Day was upon them. To express her love Marie bought Melvin a Valentine's Day Card and cooked him a fabulous dinner. He tore the card to pieces and then threw it in her face. As Marie cried he yelled out to her, "This card; just like you, are worthless to me." Marie couldn't understand his negative behavior, so she watched him clown in silence. He then pushed their Valentine's dinner from the table to the floor, got up and walked right through it. Marie was devastated. She had taken all day to plan a romantic evening with her new husband.

Shortly after Marie got married, I noticed a major change in her attitude and self-esteem. She would call me and as she talked she whispered lower and lowers on the phone. Each time I asked her to meet with me somewhere she could talk without fear she would say, "He'll know if I leave the house." Now, I must admit, "this was really weird to me, because I had never experienced this type of behavior before."

As I thought back, before they were married there were other times Marie was belittled by Melvin. There was the time that Marie let Melvin use her car. He took her car and later that same day he arrived home without it. He was yelling, screaming and throwing things around. He blamed her for the car breaking down on him. So to get even with her and "*the car*," he left it on the side of the road. He told Marie he had it towed to the car repair shop.

Marie believed him and waited for more than four months on her car to be repaired. Every time she asked him what shop her car was in or when it was going to be repaired he procrastinated and put her off. He constantly told her she was dumb for keeping the piece of junk anyway. After five months of waiting for her car to be repaired Melvin finally told Marie he had it junked.

She stayed with him, but, was feeling bad about herself because he would often tell her, his bad luck was because of her. Marie would often say, "I love him because he makes me see the stupid things I do," "I need him in my life because he's so organized," "He brought me into his life when I needed him most."

All of these statements are statements of low-esteem. Melvin had repeatedly told her she was no good, worthless and undeserving. Because of his statements she began feeling this way. He did and said so many negative things to her that she began to believe them. Her affirmations were destructive instead of constructive. As I worked to convince Marie to seek counseling for this problem she finally got enough strength to consider it.

Use Affirmations for Recovery

She was so afraid to leave the house that all she could do without feeling threatened was talk to herself. When he wasn't around she recited her affirmations aloud. When he was present she said them silently. Affirmations helped begin Marie's road to recovery even though she was unsure about where she was headed. The use of affirmations helped Marie gain enough strength and confidence to get out of a bad relationship. She literally talked her way out the bad relationship by reciting positive things to herself.

There are many times during your day affirmations can be put to work. You can repeat positive statements while riding in the car, taking a walk, washing dishes, feeding the children, using the restroom or taking a coffee break. It's best to repeat your affirmations before going to sleep, and again upon waking.

Some people use prayer and Scriptures as their affirmations. You can write them or say them aloud, which ever will help make your personal message sink in.

Remember to Use Reminders

Reminders help strengthen your affirmations. Reminders come in many forms and are simple ways to keep affirmations visible. By placing affirmations in visible-easy to see places you are using reminders. To do this all you have to do is write affirmations on large and small sheets of paper and place them in places that you will see them daily. Reminders should help your eyes fall naturally upon your affirmations.

Try Visualizations

Visualizations are important because once you make a conscious decision to change your behavior, you began to make the changes in those things that have unconsciously driven your past attitudes and mindsets.

If you try to make changes in your life without really visualizing the change you set yourself back by performing old patterns and mindsets. Visualizations are rehearsal for a part of your life that you want to perform on a permanent basis.

With the help of visualizations, you can convince yourself that it's okay to achieve your goals. You began to open yourself up to the numerous ways you can get or make things happen.

Here are eight ways to draw upon personal strength through affirmations, self-talk, reminders or visualizations.

1. Know what behavior you want to change.

Create a mental image of how you want to act in a particular situation. Don't be afraid to see yourself going through the motions to make behavioral changes. Be completely satisfied with your efforts before you end visualization. You'll begin to like your new and better self.

2. **Select a quiet, uninterrupted place to think.**

   Completely relax your body so that your full attention is on the mental pictures that you've created. Breath slowly, taking deep breaths and relax even more as you breathe. When you relax your visualizations become clear and more acceptable.

3. **Perform behaviors as you want them performed.**

   Make every aspect of your visualization so real that you feel the presence of being there. Feel emotions that you would feel as if it were happening. Let your body feel the physical sensations and if there is conversation, mentally speak the words that you would say. Bring details to the forefront making your self-talk as real and as complete as you possibly can. (See Relaxation Techniques)

4. **Hold negative emotions as long as you can.**

   Let your emotions carry over into the next day. Feel the sensations of achieving your goals for long lengths of time.

6. **Repeat these steps at least five times a day.**

   Bring each of your goals, affirmations and dreams into reality with visualizations and, before you know it, your goals will be met and your dreams will come true.

7. **Don't rush things.**

   When you start small you learn to visualize better over a shorter period of time. Starting small also keeps you from becoming overwhelmed.

8. **Be realistic.**

   To become more effective with your visualizations and affirmations they should be believable, attainable ideas based on reasonable and humanly possible goals. Avoid fantasies and stick with realistic goals that you are almost sure to meet. Be sure to set yourself in motion right away to work toward achieving your goals.

9. **Don't expect overnight miracles.**

   It took many years for you to get to your present condition with your mindsets, and conditioning. It is unreasonable to demand total reversal on your mindset patterns by the next day. Allow time for your new beliefs and expectations so that you can integrate them into the newer and updated beliefs.

A Moving Thought

Every day you must remind yourself of your own ability; and how good your mind is. Affirm that you can make something really good out of life.

Chapter 17

Mindset 16: Committing to Commitments

In this chapter you will learn how to honor your commitments until the job or task is done.

Making Commitments That Last

One day I caught one of my friends in the mood to talk about herself. I met her for lunch and she invited me into her office afterwards. Her office was very comfortable and furnished with handsome artifacts and vibrant colors that blended well together.

The relationship she had with her co-workers seemed to be perfect. A spirit of good will cloak her entire company. As I looked around her office I noticed a beautiful huge highly polished marble desk. On it sat a tattered, torn and very used bible. It was the only *old* object that I could find in this ultra-modern office. I decided to comment on this wonderful inconsistency. She told me a very simple, but effective secret.

"That book" she replied pointing to the tattered bible, is the most up-to-date thing in this entire building. She then pointed to a lady feeding a baby in an office next to her. She said, "See that lady feeding her baby?" Her baby is only six weeks old, she returned to work with her baby in hand. This book is newer to me than that newborn baby is. Equipment wears out, furnishing styles change, babies grow up, but this book is so far ahead of us, it never gets out of date.

What Do Your Commitments Mean To You?

If we take a look at official definitions, commitment can mean several different things. For example, *to be entrusted to*, *to confide in*, *deliverance from or to something*, *surrendering*, *submission*, *yielding*, *pledging*, *making a covenant*, *promising*, *giving ones word*, *meeting an obligation*, *taking responsibility*, *undertaking*, *attesting to*, *making a choice or making a determination*. Whew!

How, many times in our lives have we found ourselves in a place similar to these requirements? We take on a job, we have a child or get married, things that are usually outside of ourselves, though they have a great impact on what goes on inside of us.

When I ask potential clients if they are 100% committed to doing 'change work' I often get a "yes, definitely", however there are times I get a confused look. Let's look at it this way.

- If you weren't 100% committed to breathing, what would happen?
- If you are not 100% committed to changing your life what do you think would continue to happen?
- What would happen if you did commit to changing your life?
- What would happen if you didn't?

Commit to Understanding the Message

She added by saying when I left home to strike out on my own, my mother gave me this bible with the suggestions that if I read and practiced its teachings, I would learn how to get through life successfully. At the time mom gave it to me, I only took the bible to humor her. For years I never looked at it, it just sat in a corner on a table in my bedroom. I didn't think I needed it. Well she continued ... "To say the least I was a fool to think such a thing. I was stupid and then one day I look up and my life was in a mess."

"Everything went wrong primarily because I was wrong, doing wrong and living wrong." I succeeded at many things, but I also failed at more things than I'd like to remember. I realized after numerous failures my troubles were due to my lack of commitment. I wasn't committed to my job, my family, my friends, or my life. I debated and griped about everything people had to say. I'm surprised that anyone liked me.

"One night while going through old boxes I came across that old-forgotten bible. It brought memories of what my mother had told me when she gave it to me, so I began to read it every day. I actually studied it aimlessly. It was so strange how things began to happen for me the moment I began to read it. In a flash everything became different. The more I read the more I learned. Then one day a message jumped right off the page as I was reading. It changed my life - and when I say changed it, it really did change it. Ever since I read that sentence everything has changed for the better for me."

"What is this wonderful messgae I asked?" She quoted it slowly for me, "Wait on the Lord: be of good courage, and he shall strengthen thine heart; wait I say on the Lord." (Psalm 27:14)

"I don't know why that one line has affected me so much she went on to say, but it did. Something happened to me when I read it; I guess you could say I had a spiritual revelation.

My thoughts shifted from negative to positive and that day I decided to put my faith in God and do my best trying to follow the principles outlined in the bible. As I changed my thoughts I began to think differently and I was gradually remade. So the story of this new thinking woman was concluded. She altered her thinking, which in turn altered her failure status and now her life is more successful.

This incident illustrates an important fact about human nature: you can think your way through failure and unhappiness if you are committed. Your success rate is determined by thoughts that mindsets that occupy your mind. So it's proven in the famous words of Ralph Waldo Emerson, "A man is what he thinks about all day long."

Commit To a Better Life

To become dedicated to finding success in your life you must remain committed. Remaining positive is a simple form of commitment. Rising above your present situation and finding the possibilities in a bad situation is also a form of commitment. There is power in making the commitment to improve your life. When you dedicate yourself to rising above your circumstances, you are able to rise to any occasion. Once you let people around you know you want more out of life you become more dedicated to getting it. They buy into your vision and become your cheering section and you their champion.

This sense of commitment is somehow always rewarded. It's a part of the human spirit. People like to witness success. It makes them feel that anything is possible. It feels good to the person observing and it opens the door to help the onlooker feel a sense of success as well. Commitments help you strive for the life and lifestyle you desire. By committing yourself to your dreams, goals and desires you dedicate yourself to someday having a better life.

Commit To Put In More Than You Get Out

When you make a commitment across the board to heal your life, you usually get very positive results. The more you put in, the more you will get out. In the gathering of results you also find that you become truly empowered. And it is empowerment that comes from a very deep place within you, that's defined by you. Ultimately it really is all about you!

Here's how you put more in so you can get more out of it.

- Exhibit the type of confidence that will help attract attention and advance further and faster in your career.
- Meet challenges head on as you prepare for a better life.
- Raise your expectations in life so that you can live better.
- Get a handle on your life as you build your ladder of success.

- Believe that *you can* do all the things that will help you get what you want from life.
- Develop a plan that will help you create magic in your life so you'll appreciate, approve, respect and accept yourself.
- Build your power system by setting reachable goals.
- Make positive choices based on a healthy sense of self-worth and self-value.
- Challenge your circumstances in life so you'll become more than who really are.
- Take control of your life by taking action and taking charge of your responsibilities.
- Build better and more supportive relationships.
- Manage your problems, ideas and risks and finances.
- Become more committed to your own future and receive a better lifestyle.

Each of these mindsets is vital because you have to fully commit yourself to bettering your life if you want to rise above any difficult situations.

A commitment is not a promise to yourself that you will do something. Your commitment is something you live by day in and day out. Commitments are promises to yourself that you make and keep. Everything you do is a reflection of your commitment. Every approach you take in your life, the good times, the hard times and the successful times are expressions of commitment. True commitment is the focusing of energy toward a purpose or cause. It is doing rather than saying. It is preserving and continuing to pursue your vision in spite of distractions, hardships, criticisms, and risks. It is doing something that you believe is right for you to do. You can make a lot of mistakes on your journey through life and you can do it without jeopardizing your ability to achieve your dreams. But it will not happen if you make the mistake of failing to commit fully. No one can help you overcome the lack of commitment to your life. If you don't have it, no one can provide it for you. You must demand it from yourself.

Commit To Your Own Commitments

Keeping your own commitments is a major step in the right direction, but breaking commitments is a step backward. Try your best not to make commitments you can't keep. When you fail to keep your commitment's you also fail to move progressively toward your better life.

Before you can keep commitments with other people you must be able to keep the commitments you make to yourself. Keeping commitments help others trust and believe in you. Commitments are translated into promises, which are why people hold them so high. It assures that you will stick to something because you've given your solid word on it. When you make commitments you give your time, efforts and enthusiasm as a part of the promise.

To help you commit to your commitments try to incorporate these five steps into your life.

1. **Develop your personal talents.**

   When emotional commitment and enthusiasm are brought into your life it helps create an environment where all talents can be nurtured, developed and put to their highest use. You actually develop for your talents, not the other way around. When you are striving to better your life you automatically tap into your deepest reserves. By pulling out what is within - you begin to unleash your God-given gifts.

2. **Meet your challenges head on.**

   When you are committed to bettering yourself you accept the challenges and the difficult road ahead. You understand that challenges are there to help you grow and generate the energy you need to help you move in the right direction.

3. **Prepare for your risks.**

   Emotional commitment and enthusiasm have a positive effect on you. It gives you so much excitement you are willing to take the risks that are essential to pursuing your goals. With this commitment you see the true value involved with taking risks if it's going to help you pursue your goals. If there is something in it for you, then you are naturally more willing to take the risks.

4. Develop your excellence.

    Excellence is going beyond the call of duty, doing more than what is expected of you. By maintaining the highest standards, looking after the smallest detail and going that extra mile you can attain excellence. Excellence is doing your very best, in everything, in every way. People will drive hundreds of miles to endure a piece of excellence from their fellow man.

5. Care for others.

    Commitment inspires excellence and excellence in turn inspires others to care about your commitments. People who care about you show enthusiasm and they bring a level of excellence to your life.

You grow constantly when you renew your commitment to better yourself in all areas of your life. To have a well-rounded life you should strive to grow even after you've achieved your goals. The best things you can do is commit to developing your talents and skills.

Commitment Takes Practice

Make promises as often as possible, but remember it takes practice. Here are the basic principles for practicing commitment. One of the first things you should do is make your promises in public, before as many people as possible. Commitments create solidarity. "They make us responsible, and they permit greater degrees of personal freedom."

Build an "Identity," Not a Public "Persona".

People who have strong identities make personal commitments with such intensity that they would be willing to sacrifice something deeply important to them -- and if need be, to die - rather than give up those commitments. To build a strong identity focus on the promises made to others.

Companies know that their identities are shaped by the promises that they make, and through those promises, they develop uniqueness. A brand is a promise: FedEx promises delivery; the U.S. Post Office merely predicts delivery. What do you promise with full commitment?

Put Your Body into Your Promises.

The body never lies. We often feel more than we can see. Your body should be able to feel when things aren't right or off track or if things are moving in the wrong direction. Your body has a way of sending warning signs and signals that can help you determine when something is off.

To determine this, when you're not really sure all you have to do is … Listen to your inner voice and feel the energy you receive from it. Cultivate what has been said and then use it to accomplish your goals. Trust in what you feel and you will do the right thing. Even your most difficult times will become easier for you to handle if you learn to trust what your body is feeling.

"You can have anything you want if you are willing to give up the belief that you can't have it."

– Robert Anthony

Chapter 18

Mindset 17: Watching Out For Haters

In this section you will learn that success brings opposition and you'll be able to handle that too.

Here Comes the Opposition

On your journey to move in a direction that is beneficial and fruitful so that you can be more, enjoy more, and have more; you have to be ready for the hating opposition. When I began my professional career, I realized that no matter which way I turned there was competiveness, haters and your so-called opposers.

While on your journey you naturally go about choosing which way you're going to go, whose going to be your friend and whose going to be left out of your life. In life this is par for the course and it falls in line with the natural order of things. In life as in business and pleasure there are going to be people that are jealous, envious and as we say in today's terms -'haters.' You've got to have a few haters in order to succeed. I say make a generous toast to your haters and welcome them to your success. 'Ain't nothing like having haters. They keep you on point. They help keep you on task and they surely keep you alert. They are lurking everywhere that you are. If you are hated, there's probably a good or lousy reason why you are. Whether you deserve it or not, follow these mindsets to help you deal with the haters.

Someone Is Judging You

It doesn't matter how you choose to live your life — whether you build a business or work a corporate job; have children or choose not to have children; travel the world or live in the same town all of your life; go to the gym 5 times a week or sit on the couch every night — whatever you do, someone will judge badly you for it.

For one reason or another, someone will find a reason to project their insecurities, their negativity, and their fears onto you and your life, and you'll have to deal with it.

With that in mind, let's talk about being judged and criticized. And just for fun, I'll share some of the most hateful comments I've received. And more importantly, the strategies I use to deal with them. Here's what I've learned about dealing with the people who judge you, your work, your goals and your success.

Your Biggest Hater Is...

It's easier to complain about the outside haters, but the biggest hater in your life usually lives between your own two ears. Working up the courage to move past your own vulnerability and uncertainty is often the greatest challenge you'll face on the way to achieving your goals.

When I started my first business, it wasn't the criticism from outsiders that held me back. It was my own mind worrying that people would think I was a failure because I skipped getting a "real job" to "start some publishing company." I didn't tell most of my friends about what I was doing for almost a year because I was so worried about what they would think about it.

When I started writing, it wasn't the hurtful comments from readers that prevented me from getting started. It was my own fears about what they would think if I wrote about the things I cared about. I wrote my ideas in a plain notebook for a year before I worked up the courage to start sharing them publicly.

Those are just two examples of the types of internal fears and criticism that so often prevent us from moving toward our goals. It can take a lifetime to learn that just because people criticize you don't mean they really care about your choice to do something different. Usually, the haters simply criticize and move on. And that means that you can safely ignore them and continue doing your thing.

But that is easier said than done because we all like to be validated. Some people like it more than others, but everyone wants to be respected and appreciated to some degree. I certainly do. Whenever I choose to take a risk and share my work with the world, I wonder about what my friends will think, what my family will think, and how the people around me will see me because of that choice. Will this help my reputation? Will this hurt my reputation? Should I be worrying about my reputation?

On one hand, I believed in myself and I knew that I wanted to contribute something to the world around me. But on the other hand, I was scared that people wouldn't approve of my work and would criticize me when I started sharing the things I cared about or believed. It was more important to contribute something to the world than it was to protect myself from criticism.

The Truth about Haters

Sad to say but haters are not always attributed to the circumstances; a lot of time its other people and those people often show up as fakers. They have smiling faces that are turned upside down. There's only one positive about a hater, you cannot progress without them.

I would not give the opposition a second thought because once you address them, tweet them, email them etc, the fight is never-ending. It's just not worth your time or efforts. It's another form of distraction that takes you off your goal setting mission. Why allow anyone to interrupt your climb to the top.

My mom always said to me "Bullshit on the bullshit." Harsh but true. I never knew what she meant by this statement. I simply thought she cussed too much, but as I got older I understood it to mean don't pay attention to bullshitters, just keep on moving forward and you'll succeed.

If I paid attention to the bullshitters, I would no longer be climbing my ladder of success. She would later say as long as I'm ignoring the bullshit I'd eventually leave the bullshitters behind. While they were trying to criticize me, step on me, pull me down and talk bad about me they would be the ones who would lose their footing. They would be so busy trying to tear me down that they would slow their own progress down.

Avoid the Haters If You Want to Progress

Look at your success as being on a treadmill, every time you put one foot in front of the other you have to put the other foot in front in order to keep moving forward. You can't go backwards. The only way is forward moving actions. If you stop to pay attention to distractions you might misstep and fall off your course. When you listen or pay attention to distractions it holds you back, shortens your success ride or might even hurt you. Now you'll be spending valuable time trying to climb back on and get back to where you were. You've lost valuable progress.

This is the same way your haters take you off your path, making you miss a beat, fail or pause in your attempts to win. You cannot spend time with haters because they cause you to engage in needless thinking, and negative energy. No one succeeds when they engage in this kind of energy. They don't have the time. Haters have no significant worthiness in anyone's life.

My mom would always remind me by saying, "I don't know everything, but I know what I know." And the one thing I do know is, "Haters will hate."

One time I was going through a very trying time in my life and Gladys Knight and I spoke about it. She said, "Ella it's just a hater, don't be a doormat for anyone." You don't have time for that, it's your time. Strive for your kind of success." Don't address the hater; address your dreams and goals. That's the best way to deal with a hater. Haters want to ride on your star. Don't give them a free ride.

I've learned to be a shining star by watching Beyonce, I've never seen a girl so in control of her own life, publicity and future. She is so regal in the face of adversity. It would be so easy for her to try and defend herself, but she doesn't entertain the ignorance. She just moves along, moving forward and steady remaining one of the best entertainers in the world. She just keeps putting one foot in front of the other moving forward, making progress and succeeding. Your haters have no power over you unless you hand it to them on a silver platter. They can only feel like they've won when you help them.

Ignore the Distractions

Criticism and negativity from other people is like a wall. And if you focus on it, then you'll run right into it. You'll get blocked by negative emotions, anger, and self-doubt. Your mind will go where your attention is focused. Criticism and negativity don't prevent you from reaching the finish line, but they can certainly distract you getting to it. However, if you focus on the road in front of you and on moving forward, then you can safely get past the walls and barriers that are nearby, trying to block your success.

Focus on the Road Ahead, Not the Distractions

This is my preferred approach to haters. When someone dishes out a negative comment, use that as a signal to recommit to your work and to refocus on the road ahead of you. Some people are determined to take things personally and tear down the work of others. Your life is too short to worry about pleasing those people. Focus on the road, not the distractions.

How to Respond to Haters

Most people need love and acceptance a lot more than they need advice. If you're going to respond to your haters, then getting a response like that should be your goal.

Rather than beating the haters back with insults, win them back with sincerity. Most people don't want to be convinced that your work is wonderful; they just want to know that you care.

Where to Go From Here

I've said this many times before, but it bears repeating: I don't really have anything figured out. I'm not an expert and I don't have all the answers. I'm still learning to deal with criticism like everyone else.

There isn't a month that goes by that someone doesn't have something to say about Ella Patterson. I have no problem accepting criticisms or facing the music. I haven't been a perfect angel. I decided years ago after losing almost everything that I would not let anyone define who I was and how I was going to move in a more positive direction. People can say anything about me, but in the end it is me who decides what will and what will not hurt me or define me.

Here's what I can summarize about dealing with haters. People who are miserable and hurting will spit out harmful things about others just to remove the attention from their own struggles. Some days we can take the verbal punishment better than other days. So with that said, here's my question:

How do you move in the right direction when there are so many haters lurking?

____

____

How can you remove yourself from the negativity of others?

____

____

1. Don't Be the Hater

Don't be the person who tears down someone else's hard work. The world needs more people who contribute their gifts and share their work and ideas. Working up the courage to do that can be tough. Support the people who display that courage.

2. Don't Let Haters Block Your Vision

If you're dealing with criticism, focus on the path ahead. Another way I heard it put recently, "Ignore the person that yells the loudest. They usually come from the cheap seats."

3. Surprise Haters with Kindness

If you choose to respond to the haters, then surprise them with kindness. You might just win a new supporter.

4. Make the Proper Choices

Make the choices that are right for you. People will criticize you either way.

5. Don't Make a Huge Deal Out Of It

Avoid making it look as though it hugely affects you. This shows that you are better than being influenced by others' feelings toward you. Be gentle with yourself.

6. Figure out Why You're Disliked

If it's a good reason, think about how you should change...do you need to become a better person? Some ideas to help you change might be, do small acts of kindness. Also try not to lie and always tell the truth even if it hurts.

7. If It's a Stupid Reason

If (e.g. a group of people hate you because you're smarter), then ignore it. You don't need to react to spiteful feelings towards you.

8. Speak To a Close Friend about It

When and if it gets out of control having someone to speak to can make dealing with it a whole lot easier.

9. Be Calm When Dealing With Your 'Haters'

Don't be mean, but don't be too friendly either. If they confront you about their feelings, just 'show' you don't care. There are more people in the world than them. In most cases, that 'awkward' atmosphere can be resolved by keeping physical and social distance from the person\group that hates you. Make sure to be 'positive' and 'relaxed' when doing this, so it's less emotionally demanding for you. If the hating started after a specific event, you need to give time for the dust to 'settle down'.

10. You Can't Change Yourself

If people hate you for being YOU that's the worst reason of all. There's a simple yet effective perspective for this: social relationships, be them friendly or romantic, aren't supposed to be arduous. They're supposed to be naturally fun and engaging. This is the ultimate reference when deciding who is worth your time.

11. People Are Mean Sometimes

- Always remember to stay strong. Strength in characters always defeats strength in numbers.
- Be happy with yourself. We are all born with certain talents-find your talents.
- Remember, it is not your problem if you are hated. (Well, it may be, depending on what kind of person you are). If people have such a problem with you, they should be mature enough to leave you alone.
- If the hate is against your gender, sexual orientation, religion or race, it should be ZERO tolerance and be taken up with the authorities to be.
- Do not provoke hate. Do not act stuck-up or obnoxious.
- Next time someone flips you off or swears at you, give them the peace sign.

- Remember that it could very likely be your fault. People are mean, so take that into account before you do anything that could provoke hate.
- You can tell a lot about yourself from the number of enemies you have, and the number of friends you have. Weigh the two against each other.

Warnings

- Do not seek revenge. It will very likely bite you back. If you feel that vengeance is worth the personal toll, seek help.
- Do not get in fights. This is a good way to get in trouble with the the law.

"The only thing a person can ever really do is keep moving forward. Take that big leap forward without hesitation, without once looking back. Simply forget the past and forge toward the future."

- Alyson Noel

A Moving Thought

Don't dwell on what went wrong. Instead, focus on what to do next. Spend your energies on moving forward toward finding answers.

- Dennis Waitley

Chapter 19

Mindset 18: Unloading the Dead Weight

In this section, you will learn why it's best to let go of the mess in order to become your best.

It's An Elimination Process

If you want to soar and move on to better things, you have to give up the things that weigh you down – which is not always as obvious and easy as it sounds.

Life is all about continuous progress: the ability to move forward and to achieve greatness. You cannot hope to ever achieve such things if you are holding on to things from your past.

All this does is prevent you from reaching your full potential. By holding on to past ideals or carrying extra weight you are self-sabotaging any progress you hope to make. You need to make peace with your past and learn to accept things the way they are, whether it makes sense or not. Coming to peace with certain realities is what will allow you to move on from the past in order to have a great future.

Once you let go of the things in life that are weighing you down, the quicker you will be able to achieve your goals. You need to give up certain things in order to fully commit yourself to the life you want to obtain.

Start eliminating your concern regarding the following issues and see what a difference that will make in your life.

The Opinions of Others

People know your name, not your story. They've heard what you've done, but not what you've been through. So take their opinions of you with a grain of salt. In the end, it's not what others think, it's what you think about yourself that counts. Sometimes you have to do exactly what's best for you and your life, not what's best for everyone else.

Get Past the Past

You will fail sometimes, and you understand that failure is sometimes an exercise in learning that's okay. The faster you accept this, the faster you can move onward and get on with being brilliant. Your past does not equal your future. You may not have an impact on the current moment, but remember that all that matters is what you do now.

Decide What You Want

You will never leave where you are until you decide where you would rather be. It's all about finding and pursuing your passion. Neglecting passion blocks creative flow. Energy is everything when it comes to being successful. Make a decision to figure out what you want, and then pursue it passionately.

Fulfill Goals That Matter To You

There are two primary choices in life: to accept conditions as they exist, or accept the responsibility for changing them. Follow your intuition. Don't give up trying to do what you really want to do. When there is love and inspiration, you can't go wrong.

Whatever it is you want to do, do it now. There are only so many tomorrows. Trust me, in a year from now, you will wish you had started today.

Choose To Do Something

You don't get to choose how you are going to die, or when. You can only decide how you are going to live, right now. Every day is a new chance to choose a better way of life. Change your perspective. Choose to flip the switch in your mind from negative to positive. Choose to turn on the light and stop wondering aimlessly in the dark. Choose to do work that you are proud of. Choose to truly LIVE, right now. Choose something or lose.

Don't Run From Problems that You Should Fix

Why make life harder than it has to be. The difficulties started when… conversations became texting, feelings became subliminal, sex became a game, the word 'love' fell out of context, trust faded as honesty waned, insecurities became a way of living, jealously became a habit, being hurt started to feel natural, and running away from it all became our solution. Stop running! Face these issues, fix the problems, communicate, appreciate, forgive and LOVE the people in your life who deserve it.

Life is a continuous exercise in creative problem solving. A mistake doesn't become a failure until you refuse to correct it. Long-term failures are the outcome of people who make excuses instead of decisions.

Seek Positive Points in Your Life

What you see often depends entirely on what you're looking for. When you stay stuck in regret of the life you think you should have had, you end up missing the beauty of what you do have. You will have a hard time ever being happy if you aren't thankful for the good things in your life.

Other People's Opinion

This is something far too many people worry about. This is inherently problematic, as you cannot change someone else's opinion. Everyone is entitled to his or her own opinion even if you do not agree with it or it's completely inaccurate. You just have to concentrate on living the best possible life for yourself that you can. People who engage in incessant gossip are unhappy with their own lives so they seek to degrade others to try and enhance their self-worth. The kicker is that this will leave them just as miserable as before.

Some Things Will Never Make Sense

At one point or another, you are going to realize that sometimes there just isn't a reasonable explanation as to why something occurred the way it did. You can spend all the time you want rehashing things in your mind, trying to make sense of a situation, but honestly you may never come to a realization. This is something that takes a lot of time and experience to realize, but once you do, it really can make all the difference.

Expectations

The sooner you stop expecting people to act in certain ways, the happier you will be. Allow yourself to be pleasantly surprised by the actions of others instead of becoming disappointed when they don't follow through in the manner in which you thought they would. You can only control your actions, not those of others, so it's simply in your best interest to let people act the way they will without creating false hope.

Everyone Makes Mistakes

The past is over and if you have done all you can do to make up for your mistakes, then there is nothing else you can do at this point. If people throw this in your face, then you need to cut these people out of your life. It's as simple as that. Everyone makes mistakes; it's a part of growing up. As long as you correct your mistakes and learn from them, then that should be all there is to it.

Use Your Experiences To Grow

Just because it didn't work out with one person doesn't mean it won't work out with someone else. Rather than allowing your past to pull you down and harmfully impact your future, use your experiences to grow and learn about yourself.

The people you meet in life come at the time they do for a reason. Don't waste your time replaying incidents over and over in your head trying to make sense of them. If your relationship didn't work out, it's okay, take it as a lesson learned and carry that into your future.

Don't Hold Grudges

There is no reason to actively resent another person. It doesn't harm the other person as much as it will harm you. Why are you focusing your energy on someone you don't even care about? Do you really think they are wasting their valuable time concerning themselves with your actions? Just let it be - don't engage in malicious behavior, you are beyond that. Leave whatever happened to cause this tension in the past and move on with your life. Now be happy and celebrate the new and better you.

Appreciate What You Have

Instead of focusing on what you think you are missing from your life, try and focus on what you are so fortunate to have. It's far too easy to look around at the people you surround yourself with and become jealous of what they have. Everyone is fighting a battle within that no one knows about. Just because someone has materialistic possessions does not mean he or she is internally happy. Be grateful for the things that are most important to you and relish them instead of focusing on what you believe to be missing. You have made it this far, so wouldn't it only make sense that you have everything you need?

Do Not Make Excuses

You have to seize each opportunity that is presented to you and immerse yourself completely. Do not make excuses because you will only hinder your own personal progress and prevent you from achieving your goals. If you want results, you need to stop making excuses. Work hard and take advantage of all possibilities.

Have Confidence

By this time in your life, there really is no reason to be insecure. Don't consume yourself with worry about what other people are thinking — chances are they are way more concerned with themselves than you. Everything you have done up until this point is enough and has gotten you to this place in your life. Confidence is a state of mind; if you believe you are a good person with good values, then it should be enough to build your confidence. Insecurity is something that holds people back more than anything else and it's a damn shame because the person making you feel the most insecure is yourself.

Refuse to Entertain Drama

The only thing dealing with drama will lead to is anxiety. Why are people drawn to this? I honestly don't understand. You need to surround yourself with people who are constantly pushing themselves for the better, if you are consistently surrounding yourself with negative people, this will only hinder your progression. Think back to all of the drama you have dealt with in your life and think about if it really has any effect on your life now. The answer to that question is usually no and the time put into dealing with that drama is just not worth it.

A Moving Thought

Take baby steps and don't give up! Keep moving in the right direction. Trust yourself and your abilities. Just because something didn't yet work out as planned, doesn't mean it won't work out. There is always a way and you can't lose unless you give up.

Chapter 20

Mindset 19: Improving Financial Health

This chapter will help you get your financial health in order

Create a Financial Budget

It's all about saving the money you earn by banking smart, and using your banking for financial growth. The earning power of women has increased significantly over the past decade, but saving money should be an important part of every woman's life, no matter what her income level is. And whether you're new to saving money or just want some "back to the basics" ideas, here's help. There are certainly a lot of ways to tackle the subject of saving money. Starting with these steps is a common way to launch a lifetime of successful saving.

Create a Realistic Budget

Budgeting is a logical pairing to tracking your spending when your goal is saving money. And just like your method of keeping tabs on spending, budgeting can be as simple or as complicated as you need it to be. Whether you use notebook paper or sophisticated personal finance software, a combination of both or anything in between, your goal is to decide where your money is going to go each month - and stick with it.

Keep a Spending / Saving Journal

There's no way to know how much money you are truly spending unless you track it. Most every bank gives you online access to your everyday accounts, so carefully review this information as you begin to take charge of where your money goes. You can also find spending journal spreadsheet templates or smartphone apps that help; the bottom line is to find a system that works for you.

Save Your Money

You need to put away the largest portion. Not just a 10% or so but 30% or 40%. It is possible to do that and still live a very comfortable life. Some women live beyond their means and end up with nothing but memories of that nice sports car or that fancy apartment. Live within your means; base your spending around what you would make at a good entry-level job.

What to Do With Your Saved Money

So what to do with the money you save? Well, set enough aside to pay for all of your expenses: food, housing, tuition, utilities, car, whatever for 4 months. This is your emergency fund, put it in your saving account and don't spend it. The rest you should invest. Invest for at least 5 years and probably 10. Mutual funds are low maintenance and are well suited for this. I strongly advise against investing in individual stocks. Few people are able to make money off buying and selling individual stocks. Stick with mutual funds; they are safer and more reliable (at least for the novice investor).

The Best Investments

The best possible investment you can make is an education. With a nice big nest egg and a good degree you can do just about anything you want when you retire. Without education or any job skills that money will eventually be gone. With an education you can make the most of your savings, use it as capital for your own business or invest it for a steady source of income.

Open a CD account

A certificate of deposit (CD) is a solid, time-honored and low-risk way of saving money. Just remember - you usually can't withdraw funds from a CD until it matures without paying an early withdrawal penalty. The Ally Bank No Penalty CD is one exception. It allows you to withdraw your entire balance without a penalty - earned interest included - any time after the first six days of funding your account (this initial six day period is required by federal banking regulation). Generally, the longer the term, the more interest you earn with traditional CDs that have early withdrawal penalties. Balance your goal of earning interest against the timeliness of your need to use the cash elsewhere.

Get Better Rates

Certificates of deposit (CDs) offer some of the best guaranteed rates on your money and are insured up to $250,000 each. The catch: you have to lock up your money for three months to five years or more. If interest rates fall before the CD expires, the bank is out of luck and must give you the rate it quoted. If rates climb, you're stuck with the lower rate. Also online bank and money market accounts can be an attractive option, too. They can pay more than banking accounts and you don't have to lock up your money for a specific amount of time.

Saving for Retirement

Regardless of how you see life in your "golden years," it's going to take money to make it happen. And unlike some of life's unexpected expenses, it's practically a certainty that you're going to continue to get older and still need income, whether you continue to work or live off your hard-earned savings. Either way, participating in a 401(k) plan or another type of employer-sponsored retirement plan is usually a solid way to start saving money for your long-term needs - if for no other reason than the potential tax advantages.

Money in a Bank Account is Safe

A bank is one of the safest places to stash your cash. It is far better than stashing under the mattress. The federal government increased the level of insurance on bank accounts -- it's now $250,000 per depositor. Don't forget that you pay for the convenience of a bank account.

Banks generally pay lower rates on interest-bearing accounts than brokerages and mutual fund companies that offer check-writing privileges. What's more, bank fees can be high -- account costs can easily add up to $200 a year or more unless you keep a minimum required balance on deposit.

Inflation Can Eat What You Earn From a Bank

Even at a low rate of inflation, the annual creep in the cost of goods and services usually outpaces what banks pay in interest-bearing accounts.

Not All Interest Rates are Created Equal

Banks frequently use different methods to calculate interest. To compare how much money you'll earn from various accounts in a year, ask for each account's "annual percentage yield." Banks typically quote both interest rates and APYs, but only APYs are calculated the same way everywhere.

ATM Fees Take a Huge Bite Out of Your Budget

The convenience of using automated teller machines is an increasingly pricey one. On average, the fee your bank charges you to use another institution's ATM is $2.00. That's on top of the fee that the other institution will charge you to use its ATM.

Getting the Best Deal Takes Work

You won't get a great deal on a car if you just walk into a dealer and plunk your money down. Likewise, you won't get a great banking deal unless you comparison-shop and ask about price breaks. For example, a bank might offer free checking if you are a shareholder or if you direct deposit your paycheck.

Use the Internet to Shop for Bank Services

You can use the Internet to compare fees, yields, and minimum deposit requirements nationwide. Sites like Bankrate.com allow you to search and compare the highest yields and the lowest costs on banking, savings, loans and deposit rates nationwide. You can search by geographic location or use CNNMoney.com loan center.

Banking Online Can Make Bill-Paying Easier

Electronic bill-paying can save you the monthly hassle of paying your bills. And if you couple online banking with a personal-finance management program, such as Quicken or Microsoft Money, you'll be able to link your banking with your budgeting and financial planning as well. But be careful. Some vendors warn the consumer of price hikes in the fine print of a bill.

You Can Bank Without a Bank

A number of financial institutions offer accounts that resemble bank services. The most common: Credit union accounts; mutual funds, money market funds; and brokerage cash-management accounts. Of course, saving money isn't as much a matter of gender as it is a matter of understanding come basic ideas that almost always work. The important thing is to have a plan and to execute that plan while tracking your results so you can make adjustments as necessary.

Create a Reasonable Budget

Creating a budget is an essential first step to taking control of your money. Many discover they're spending far more than they realized, while a lucky few pat themselves on the back for saving more than they knew. Once you create a budget, you'll see the areas in which you can cut costs. Learn how much you can save each month toward your future goals, and then understand how to divide those savings among your short-term and long-term goals.

1. Budgeting is very necessary.

Get a grip on your spending - and to make sure your money is being used the way you want it to be used.

2. Budgeting requires three steps.

Identify how you're spending money now. Evaluate your current spending and track spending making sure it stays within those guidelines.

3. Use software to save grief.

If you use a personal-finance program such as Quicken or Microsoft Money, the built-in budget-making tools can create your budget for you.

4. Don't drive yourself nuts.

One drawback of monitoring your spending by computer is that it encourages overzealous attention to detail. Once you determine which categories of spending can and should be cut (or expanded), concentrate on those categories and worry less about other aspects of your spending.

5. Watch out for cash leakage.

If withdrawals from the ATM machine evaporate from your pocket without apparent explanation, it's time to keep better records. In general, if you find yourself returning to the ATM more than once a week or so, you need to examine where that cash is going.

6. Spending beyond your limits is dangerous.

Many households with total income of $50,000 or less are spending more than they bring in. This doesn't make you an automatic candidate for bankruptcy - but it's definitely a sign you need to make some serious spending cuts. Be more aware of your true spending limits.

7. Beware of luxuries dressed up as necessities.

Don't fool yourself into thinking that the things you're buying are necessary. Check yourself. Do you want it or do you need it? If your income doesn't cover your costs, then some of your spending is probably for luxuries - even if you've been considering them for filling a real need.

8. Tithe yourself.

Aim to spend no more than 70% of your income. That way, you'll have the other 30% left to save..

9. Don't count on windfalls.

When projecting the amount of money you can live on, don't include dollars that you can't be sure you'll receive, such as year-end bonuses, tax refunds or investment gains. It's best not to count it as spendable money. Count it as money you'll put aside if and whenever they come in.

10. Beware of spending.

As your annual income climbs from raises, promotions and smart investing don't start spending for luxuries until you're sure that you're staying ahead of inflation. It's better to use those income increases as an excuse to save more.

Know the Basic Tax Facts

As you begin to make money you need to at least know the basic tax facts. I am not an accountant, but there are several things I learned after filing for bankruptcy that if I had known them I would have not had tax problems. Know some brief facts about our tax system and how you fit in. As you embark on your own annual tax odyssey you might be surprised about who pays what, who doesn't pay, according to recent IRS statistics.

- A big refund check means too much is withheld.

  In effect, you're giving the government an interest-free loan.

- Too little withheld, may get underpayment penalty.

  You must pay 90% of what you owe for the tax year by the end of that year or an amount equal to 100% of your tax liability for the previous tax year, whichever is smaller.

- Not all taxable income is taxed at the same rate.

  That's because portions of your earned income fall into different brackets, which are assigned different tax rates. Generally speaking, the first dollar you make will be taxed at a lower rate than your last dollar. Your marginal tax rate is the tax bracket at which the highest (or last) portion of your income is taxed.

- If tax is owed on *income: investments, CDs, money markets.*

  Your combined bracket is the sum of your top (or marginal) federal tax rate and your top state income tax rate. It may be less if you itemize deductions since you will be able to deduct your state income tax on your federal return.

- If you don't pay tax by April 15, you may receive a penalty.

  An extension allows you to file your return after the due date. But full payment is still required by April 15. If you make a partial payment by then, you may be charged interest on the amount outstanding.

- You can reduce your chances of being audited.

One of the best ways is to fill out your return completely, correctly, and on time every year.

- Pay estimated taxes if you're self-employed

Expect hefty investment income or profits from a property sale; or if you don't have enough taxes withheld to cover the taxes you'll owe on non-wage-related income. Consider paying them if they haven't opted for voluntary withholding on their pension or IRA payments. Estimated taxes are due four times a year (April 15, June 15, Sept. 15, and Jan. 15).

- Adjusted gross income is the total income minus certain "above the line" deductions:

Your AGI primarily determines whether or not you're eligible for tax breaks. Almost every break, be it a deduction, exemption, or a credit, has its own AGI limit.

- Taxable income is AGI minus exemptions and deductions.

The less your taxable income, the less in taxes you'll owe. That's why it's in your best interest to take advantage of tax breaks where you can.

- **A credit is better than a deduction.**

  A credit is a dollar-for-dollar reduction of the taxes you owe. A $100 credit means you pay $100 less in taxes. A deduction reduces the taxes you owe by a percent of every dollar you're allowed to deduct. You calculate the worth of your deduction by multiplying your marginal (or top) tax rate by the amount of the deduction. If you're in the 25% tax bracket, a $100 deduction means you'll pay $25 less in taxes (0.25 times $100).

You can't tax business. Business doesn't pay taxes. It collects taxes."

- Ronald Reagan

Chapter 21

Mindset 20: Reward Yourself by Relaxing!

In this chapter you will explore ways to relax and why relaxation techniques are best for beginning and ending your day.

Enjoy the Beauty of Your Rewards

Most of us do not work because we have to, we work because we need money to survive. The problem is work is sometimes all we do. We forget that life is more than work. Life is also about balance. In order to have a balanced life we must do more than work. What about having some good ole fashion fun? We need fun and laughter to keep our minds off our problems.

How about rest? Not just sleeping to get ready for the next day's work, but resting the body and mind from all activity. What about solitude? Take an hour or perhaps a day from the hustle and bustle of life and people. It's called a mental health break.

Let us not forget that our bodies and minds need relaxation. Relaxation helps to keep the gray matter upstairs (our brains) from getting overwhelmed. Work is necessary, but it is not the only thing required to succeed. All work and no relaxation may give us a balanced checkbook, but it will also give us an unbalanced mind.

There are many benefits ahead when you learn to relax your body and mind. As you try relaxation exercises, allow oxygen to fill your lungs, letting your diaphragm expand downward toward your abdomen. When properly done, your tummy will actually begin to expand outward. Forget holding your tummy in for the time you are doing these exercises, just relax and enjoy. If you notice your shoulders rising or your chest expanding you're probably breathing incorrectly. Try again, this time, just remember to focus and relax. Here are some rewarding relaxation techniques.

Relaxation 1: Let go; get rid of your worries.

While relaxing, imagine you have an empty box. This is the box that you will put all your worries into. As you put your worries in this box imagine them disappearing from your life. See yourself placing all your worries in this box, especially those worries you've been neglecting because they are too large or too painful to think about. Go ahead put them all in the worry box. Now walk away from the box and as you walk away let them dissolve inside the box. Feel the pleasure of being light and carefree. Now gently come out of your relaxation and feel free of your problems.

Relaxation 2: Treat yourself better.

While relaxing comfortably picture yourself in your mind looking good and feeling good. Let go of any upsetting feelings and thoughts that are holding you back. Let go, right now. Think of all the little things you can do to like yourself more and then be nicer to yourself. Think of things that will make your day go smoother and make you feel more fulfilling. Think of and do things that will make your life more fun.

Relaxation 3: Choose to think positive thoughts.

While relaxing comfortably imagine all unhealthy thoughts leaving your mind. See your positive thoughts take their proper place. Identify any unhealthy thoughts so that you can change them immediately. Knowing that you can bring these thoughts into your mind each time you need them is power. After thinking for a while come out of your relaxation and take the steps you need to move toward your positive thoughts. You are ready, so don't be afraid.

Relaxation 4: Find your greatness with success.

While relaxing comfortably, see yourself looking great, feeling good, being calm and gaining enthusiasm. Notice no matter how small your accomplishments - you have a lot going for you. It has been working for you all the time you just didn't focus on the positives of it all. Look at how rich your life is right now and see the richness come in your future. See your anger toward a particular person shaking out like leaves and dissolving into nothing. See yourself moving forward, supercharged with your own life's energy. Dream of your success and it will become reality for you. As you imagine possible greatness and happiness awaiting you to take it - relax, open your eyes and turn your goals into reality.

Relaxation 5: Your personal intuitions.

While relaxing comfortably picture in your mind looking at how you plan to spend tomorrow and then consider if this is spending your time in the most valuable way. As you think about your time being spent better - make any adjustments you can to boost your self-esteem and personal intuition.

Relaxation 6: Let go of your stress.

While relaxing comfortably picture yourself without stress and tension in your body. See yourself as calm, relaxed and sure of yourself. Picture yourself looking centered and revitalized. Remind and reassure yourself that you are capable and able to handle any challenge. Be open to answers as you listen to yourself, and your personal intuition. Be aware that you may hear your answers later. As you hear them write them down.

Relaxation 7: Welcome change opportunities.

While relaxing comfortably think of the changes you would like to see; then see yourself handling this change in a positive way. Picture yourself taking the needed steps to move forward and arriving to a place in your life that's beneficial, rich and satisfying. Daydream and imagine you are successful, happy and living a wonderful and long awaited lifestyle. Take your time and don't rush it. Welcome opportunities that you've always wanted.

Relaxation 8: Strengthen beliefs and values.

While relaxing comfortably take a couple of deep breaths and as you exhale let your relaxation move slowly throughout your body. As you breathe in think of those things that you doubt about yourself. While exhaling let go of your doubts. Notice what it feels like when you believe in you. Trust yourself to be able to handle any situation. An important part of valuing yourself is listening to yourself. Remember what it feels like to be happy, relaxed and satisfied with your life. Believe that you have a right to be happy.

Relaxation 9: Let go of your fears.

While relaxing comfortably feel the fears and the hurt you've felt dissolving without trying to analyze them. Without trying to work out in detail what you're going to do, ask for help, support and guidance. Feel the connection of your personal intuition, which helps you move forward with courage. Envision your life becoming more satisfying as you turn your fears into pleasures.

Relaxation 10: Have wonderful relationships.

While relaxing comfortably envision your life and see your relationships as fulfilling. All the things you wanted in life are at your request. Know what you really want in your relationship and decide today that you are going to work in the direction to make it happen. Recognize that with relationships there are ups and downs. Envision the ups that you want to experience. Record what you want and how you'll go about getting it. Remember to be specific.

Relaxation 11: Project goodwill.

While relaxing comfortably picture yourself relaxed and feeling good. Send out goodwill and thank you notes to any person or group of people you are going to be communicating with. Send out goodwill to family members or friends you haven't seen for a while. You'll feel better and so will they. Boosting others self-esteem will also boost yours.

Relaxation 12: Feel good about moving forward.

While relaxing comfortably picture yourself moving forward. See yourself free of the influence other people have on you. Move ahead of yourself by using your anger to propel you forward. Feel free to be successful, and satisfied with your life. Take a moment to feel all you would expect to feel when feeling joyful and successful. Imagine what it would mean to you and what it would feel like to use your anger to move forward to a more successful and joyful life.

Relaxation 13: Attract the money you want.

While relaxing your body as much as possible breathe relaxed. Imagine a beautiful scene that helps you feel a sense of safety and happiness. Feel a sense of inner security, courage and trust that you will make it through any financial problems you're having. Allow yourself to feel that you deserve greater financial abundance and you have money flowing to you. Feel sufficient money coming in, more than enough money to buy your essentials and to do all the things you've always dreamed of. See yourself doing what you need to do to make your financial success and security a reality.

Relaxation 14: Find harmony at work.

While relaxing comfortably see yourself at work in a harmonious and cooperative atmosphere, noticing that all things are going well.

See and feel the trust and cooperation. See yourself also giving and receiving support on your job. Find ways to improve your service. Be aware of what you can do and what you need to know.

Relaxation 15: Create opportunities.

While relaxing comfortably breathe normal and go mentally to a place of calm. Feel yourself drawing work, money and success toward you. Feel yourself receiving the right pay for the work you do. Imagine being at the job you love; feeling confident and enthusiastic. Use your skills to enjoy the work you are doing. Imagine your favorite job and what it would feel like to have this job. Feel yourself drawing the right job, with the right people, and the right situations. Feel and listen to your inner voice regarding what is best for you to do.

Relaxation 16: Move forward with self-esteem.

While relaxing your body comfortably see yourself secure and feeling good, looking good and your life is working for you. All the things you want to achieve you see them happening. Notice the surroundings you are in, who you're with and what you're doing. Add plenty of detail and be specific. Now go enjoy all you've worked for and live a safe, happy and fulfilling life.

Relaxation 17: Learn to let go.

One good method of relaxation that works well is to let go. Lie flat on your back and, beginning with your toes, let your body go limp. Relax from your feet all the way up to your brain. After commanding your body to relax completely isolates each part of your body and watch your muscles ease into relaxation. Move this relaxation along your torso, to your back, up your arms, through your shoulders and in your neck. Allow your forearms, fingers and ears to feel relaxed also. By then you should be well on your way to dreamland.

A Moving Thought

When one door closes another one opens, and then another one, and another one and another one....

A Moving Thought

I have been through so much - but look at me still standing strong. I could write a book about my life and it could be made into a movie. Never have used it for anybody to pity or to think I want their love – I am strong. I am beautiful because I have survived more than you could ever know... And through it all I still find the courage to love, never damaged from the past.

Chapter 22

Mindset 21: Congratulations Are In Order

In this section our final section, you will be able to see and feel that you already have the ability to succeed.

Hooray…You're Moving Forward Again!

Now that you've experienced the pitfalls of not moving forward and the benefits of *Moving in the Right Direction*, it's important for you to keep reaching upward and higher as you move forward. The most important thing you can do for yourself is … keep working toward your goals and never stop reaching your goals.

People have a tendency to think that the more money they have in their bank account the more things they will have. In the dreamers view that might be very true, But in time all the money in the world won't satisfy what is required of those who have it. The more you have the more work you have to put in. If you are lucky enough to earn lots of money you have to find ways to help others whether it's through teaching, educating, uplifting, healing, building or whatever. You have to use the money for good. If you don't God will cease your flow of the money. It is not given for you to hoard and forever save and never giving back. It is a gift for you to use to find your happiness and quite possibly bestow happiness on others. You must help others through the powers of the gift. Ask anyone who has it all and then lost it. Ask me!

If they are honest and I suspect they will be, they will attest to this principle. Any level of success is about the ability to achieve and serve through giving. Our heritage is built on the legacy of true success. Serving as a model for your children and your children's children will be a legacy of your own accomplishments.

Having thankfulness and gratitude stretches far and wide when you are seeking success. Sharing is your blessing for others

You Should Be Feeling Better

If you are excited about what you've read, then your personal and professional improvements will surely come. If you're taking steps towards your goals any lingering negative attitudes should be disappearing. Destructive behaviors should be fading away and you should be freeing yourself of pressures, bad mindsets, feelings of depression and anxiety.

You should be feeling better now … better than you were when you first began reading this book. You should feel energized and determined to have the life you desire.

Perhaps you weren't completely sure of yourself and you weren't aware of how you could change your life. Now with *Moving in the Right Direction* you've taken on a whole new attitude about being more, doing more, and getting more. You've realigned your life, beaten back your fears and discovered that you can have the life you've always dreamed of. And the most incredible thing of all is you're already seeing some of your dreams come true! Guess what, you are now moving in the right direction.

You Should Feel New Energy

Can you feel it running through your veins? This newfound power and energy will make you want to keep moving forward. Can't you feel your self-confidence pumping through your heart, mind and body? Don't you feel like you're finally able to live your dreams? Haven't you begin to expect more from yourself and those around you? Doesn't this *'New You'* feel good, right, and natural for you?

Personally, I am so enthusiastic about this movement that I dread bringing this book near close.

Can you feel your affirmations working as you visualized it happening, and now you know it's not just a dream, it's real and it's your life unfolding in wonderful and positive ways. Yes, you're doing it right now! You are living your dreams and feeling how it feels to *move-in-the-right-direction.*

By now you know that moving in the right direction is a gift that you give to yourself. Your mindset is something you reward yourself with each and every new day.

Congratulations

I congratulate you on your desire to succeed. I congratulate you on moving forward. I congratulate you on acknowledging your gift. I congratulate you on opening your mind and your eyes to new abilities and greater capabilities. I congratulate you on playing it forward.

Congratulations!

"The secret to happiness is not in doing what one likes to do, but in liking what one has to do"

- Anonymous

Afterword

A Personal Note from Ella

As **I conclude this book**, I would like to end it by sharing my own belief about why we all need to find ways to *Move in the Right Direction.* I believe the stories, checklists, strategies goals, relaxations, visualizations and so forth presented in this book will help most anyone find their way to move forward as they grow, enhance and tune up their life.

It's no coincidence that our paths have crossed. You and I started this journey together with me opening up and telling you about some of my own personal trials and tribulations. I told you how I gave in to my pain by doing many things that were not socially acceptable and considered wrong by many - from buying stolen goods to becoming a teenage mother.

I was headed for a life of turmoil and there were challenges that let me know early in life that if I didn't get it together I would be going nowhere fast. Looking back, these life changing events did not bring a great deal of confidence to me and I suspect there have been times in your life that you have experienced a great deal of pain too. You were probably asking yourself: "Who in the world am I? Why do I have all these problems?" "Why am I doing the things that I'm doing?" “Why is this happening to me?”

Unfortunate incidents and situations in our lives can make us feel like life’s journey is not worth it. It can cause us to take risks, take the wrong road; traveling in the wrong direction most of our lives. In many respects it can throw us off course and cause us to back away, never trying to improve in certain areas of our lives. Don't get me wrong; I don't ever want to go through my bad times again, they were painful. Fortunately, I've learned that those difficult and agonizing times helped me write this book so that I could help others improve in areas where they feel weak or stuck.

My goal is to help as many people as I can and keep them from going through some of the hardships I’ve gone through. Clearly, back then, I was not living the kind of life I should have been living and I found myself being pulled in all the wrong directions. The truth is my life was limited and I made so many bad decisions that I was afraid to step out of the box that I had created for myself. I felt safe in the box so that's where I stayed.

As I grew older I found that I was cheating myself, my children and the rest of my family. I wrote this book because I got tired of living the life I was living. I got tired of being routine and patternized by my own doings. Yes I said patternized…I followed so many patterns of unhappiness that I became a product of bad patterns, which later became bad mindsets.

After talking over my concerns with my husband, we jointly decided to move in a more active and positive direction in all areas of our lives. We decided that we wanted to live a life that was real and memorable, at least more memorable than the one we were already living. We wanted these memories to be happier than those we were experiencing. I began to put my plan into action so, first I would stop complaining about what I didn't have or what I had did wrong. I stop playing my 'woe is me' card every time something didn't go my way. I was on a mission to mend my personal and professional life so I got off my butt and started doing something.

My husband made the decision to begin that moment too, by doing some of the things he's always wanted to do in life. The funny thing is we talked and talked and talked, but we still played it safe and we did nothing the first few weeks. Then one day we looked at each and decided we hadn't did a thing we said we were going to do, so we dropped everything and at that moment we got off our butts and starting mapping out a plan to live a more aggressive and fruitful life.

My husband must have really been ready to make a move in the right direction because he had always wanted to play golf and before I could say, "take some classes" he was out the door and on the golf course.

My long awaited dream consisted of several things: I wanted to complete all the books I had started on, I wanted to complete my Master's degree, complete my Real Estate licensing courses and work on a job that I liked well enough to stay.

We both decided that we wanted to do things and be the people that we should have been, but realized that time had gotten in the way and now it was quickly slipping past us. We wanted to be in a different situation financially and in a different place emotionally. With that overt acknowledgement of what we really wanted and the desire to get off our butts we started more journaling and commitments. We started living our dreams and suddenly our life course began to change. We changed our mindsets.

With all our bags packed we moved to a smaller, more peaceful town south of Texas, started new jobs and embedded our lives in the world of new people, places and things. We communicated with people that had the same common goals and visions. Of course we had some unsure moments, but we knew that we had made the right move. Once we decided that we could find our happiness - making the right decisions in life came much easier. As an individual I now felt more in tune, vibrant and alive.

Suddenly everything that I desired was front and center and all I had to do was work to get it. I can assure you the work never felt like work because I was having so much fun going after my dreams. Many times I was met face to face with stumbling blocks, but they never felt like the roadblocks I had before.

Everything felt better because it *was* better. Because I was living my new life I was free of worry. It all felt so natural and right. I was now in tune with my new life - doors suddenly seem to open without effort for me. Opportunities were abundant and possibilities for me were filled with more spiritual, personal and professional advantages.

To make extra money, I began ghost writing for other people, published a quarterly magazine, wrote five new books of my own, completed my Real Estate classes and helped create initiatives for diversity-oriented companies across the world. I found new ways to create new products, do more and be more with my education and profession that I had previously lost my energy for.

I'm working on reaching all of my goals and living my dreams, but I'm also helping people all over the world discover their greatest potential too.

You can live a happier and more profitable life too. All you have to do is remember that this life we choose is filled with discovery and new opportunities. If we get out of our beds each day and reach for the stars we can make our dreams come true. We can move our lives progressively forward in many new directions that are positive, nurturing and filled with positive energy.

None of us are perfect, even though we try very hard to reach perfection. I do, however believe we are able to fulfill a measure of perfection by our mere existence on this earth. We all experience spiritual aptitude as we pass through this world. Each of us is only on loan while we are here, so I strongly believe that we should be the best of who we are while we can.

As time goes on changes become significant and better, and your results become more pleasing. It's best to start seeing and believing in the *miracle of you*. See yourself as the person you want to become instead of what you are now and watch the miracles begin. Do not cease to explore new adventures so that each day you will begin a new journey and arrive at a new place in life for the first time.

An abundance of everything you want and need in order to walk onto your path awaits you. But, first make the decision to find and walk a path of determination and fearlessness. You now have the tools to do that. And most important you know how to listen to your life so that you can make the decision to transform it.

Your transformation really begins when you connect with God, who whispers to you and guides you when you are quiet enough to listen. It comes from you when you take the time to get to know what's important to you -- embracing your natural talents and gifts. The information also comes to you daily - from people you meet with messages you need to hear. I hope you'll take action now and move forward into a life of success far greater than you've previously believed possible.

In my final attempt to help you remain focused keep these strategies in mind:

- **Take steps to move in the right direction.**

  Your path to success is a daily walk; one step at a time. It's a glorious journey, not a destination to be reached in haste.

- **Take positive action every day.**

  Your success forms as you take positive action on a daily basis. Your values and the things that matter most in your life should determine your priorities.

- **Tune up your opportunities to grow.**

  Try to stretch a little bit past your comfort zone. This will improve, increase and enhance your capacity to reach greater levels of success, joy and fulfillment. Maximize challenges and opportunity and you will become a better person.

- **Plan it and then stick with it.**

  Success comes to those who plan it and then stick with the plan. Knowing your purpose helps the plan take life and unfold into the path you have chosen. There are no shortcuts. You must remain on your path. You will never find greater success anywhere else.

It is my hope that moving in the Right Direction will help you in some small way. It is my prayer that this book will also be the answer to the most important things you could be praying, hoping and wishing for.

For me … location, career and adopting a new lifestyle were at the top of my list. For you it may be different. Your personal direction matters most when you commit to finding what it is that makes you want to reconnect with who you are in the first place.

Your personal direction helps you decide how you will rewrite your own story and then tell the truth about how you found a way to do it under your own terms and conditions. This direction matters most if it is giving you a chance to discover the truth.

Everyone's dreams, goals and desires are uniquely different and each individual knows what their particular goals mean to them. If you don't find yourself fighting for a chance to live the life you want no one else will.

So, if you're ready – I mean really ready to reach for the stars, then here's your chance to live the life you've always dreamed about, here's your chance to move in the right direction and start living. This is your time. Your life is calling you to move in the right direction and be what you were created to be.

Acknowledgements

If I tried to acknowledge all the wonderful people who have helped me get to this point in my life where I am in a position to help others move in a better direction, I would run out of paper. Let cliff note it by saying that I want to thank everyone who has had any part in any measure of my success that I have attained – there are so many of you and I want to thank each of you from the insides of my heart.

I want to thank everyone who has played a part from the stories in this book to the quotes at the beginning and ending of each chapter. I want to honor the mentors who knowingly and unknowingly helped me. Thank you, thank you, thank you!

Thank you to Martin Jr., my husband of more than thirty-five years; you have been an inspiration and supportive force in my creative and hard to understand life. Even though you never wrote one word, it is your belief and dedication that gave me the courage to step up and get back on track; back to being my authentic self instead of what others want me to be. Without your dedication and spirit of adventure I would be stuck in a life I did not want.

Thanks to my daughters Juanna and T'Juanna; both of you enlightened me at pivotal times in my life. Those times mattered more than you will ever understand. Thanks girls for keeping me grounded when I thought I was the only one going through tough times. In a world where I often ask myself "who cares" – your faith in me showed in your eyes. I pray that each of you continue to grow and become even more wonderful than you already are.

Thanks to my son Martin III, it is your tremendous belief in my ability that inspired me the most. As we walked around the block to discuss some family business your commitment to me gave me the concept of creating a road map for people who want to move in the right direction. Thanks for continuing to expect more, be more and want more for me.

Thanks you to my grandchildren; Leland, Aleyia and Marlow for being in my life and for allowing me to be in theirs.

Thank you to my brother Herbert, who stood strong and never questioned my actions. I can remember when I was a very small child; you are I were like Mutt and Jeff. You have been my shoulder, my sounding block and my greatest supporter. You always saw me as a strong, determined and dedicated person, even when I doubted myself. Thanks for believing and never leaving.

Thank you to Pastor Frederick D. Haynes III, for an inspiring example you set and the tremendous spiritual growth that I have experienced through your ministry. You are my friend.

Thanks to Oprah Winfrey, who I met while riding a treadmill at the Hotel Bellaire. You said *"Keep on moving girl, just keep on moving."* You didn't know it then, but the push you gave me has helped propel me in the right direction and I'll never forget our mini conversation. That conversation was pivotal in helping me "raise the bar" so that I could assist others. Thanks for pushing me forward so that I could do God's work I love.

Thank you Salritha (Kaye) Palmer for listening when you didn't have to. I appreciate you even though I don't say it as often as I should.

Thank you Jan Miller-Rich for being a friend to the end.

Thanks to Carolyn Reidy, President of Simon and Schuster, whom I respect totally. Carolyn, you helped me believe that the universe needed my works. Our short and potent conversations were lessons that stayed with me for the past twenty years. Thanks for understanding and allowing me to remain my authentic self.

Thank you twice to the thousands of people who supported me, cheered me on and kept asking, *"When is the next book coming"*. You encouraged me to commit to the commitment and direct my efforts in a way that I could impact all people personally, professionally and spiritually.

I especially thank the strangers and supporters that I boldly asked to proof read parts of this book and for their advice so that

I could make it better for all readers. You are secret angels that God placed in my path. I am grateful for your help and expertise.

Most importantly, I thank God for using me as a vessel to deliver words of inspiration, truth and personal transformation. Thank you for expanding my territory and opening the universe for me. Thank you God for wrapping your arms around me and keeping your hands on me when I need you.

A Moving Thought

You have to come to your closed doors before you get to your open doors... What if you knew you had to go through 32 closed doors before you got to your open door? Well, then you'd come to closed door number eight and you'd think, 'Great, I got another one out of the way'... Keep moving forward.

- Joel Olsteen

Index

A Moving Thought

To find your purpose in life, there is no more valuable step than to ask one question, "What is my individual role in the Universe?"

Space for Your Notes

Using Your Movement Journal

Decide what kind of book you would like to use as your movement journal. Your movement journal can be any book you decide to use that has blank pages, such as a journal or notebook.

As you read, you'll discover more of who you are and more of what you like. As you begin to renew your thinking and spirit you'll notice a wonderful transformation that allows you to reap new benefits in life.

1. Select a great journal and label it Movement Journal.
2. Start using your Movement Journal as soon as you begin reading *Moving in the Right Direction.* Throughout this book you'll find questions that will enhance your self-exploration. Write in your journal each day, remembering that your notes are yours and will help you.
3. Don't rush your journaling process. Me-time is a precious commodity, so take time entering your thoughts. Allow yourself to think as you write proving that you and your goals are priority.

4. Use the open-ended questions that are included. These are coaching questions designed to make you think as you open your mind to the wonderful personal changes occurring.
5. Write what you are feeling in your journal. Express yourself freely.
6. Refer back to this book often. Words of encouragement are found here. Use them to bring positive thoughts to your mind as you work to improve your life.

The answers gained will keep you on track for any positive changes you want to make. The ability to change your life is in your hands. Keep in mind that this is not a contest, it is your life.

You can *always* move forward. All you need is desire. This is the key to living a good life, one that is full of joy and completeness from the inside out. I expect that this will be a wonderful time for you. I am here if you need me. Tweet me your comments @emp55

"It is always important to know when something has reached its end. Closing circles, shutting doors, finishing chapters, it doesn't matter what we call it; what matters is to leave in the past those moments in life that are over."

- Paulo Coelho,

About The Author

Ella Patterson is the author of several books: *Will The Real Women Please Stand Up! 1001 Reasons to Think Positive; Heated Pleasures, Sexual Healing, Relationship Quickies, Pampering Pleasures, and Moving in the Right Direction.*

Her books have been featured on hundreds of radio and TV shows throughout the United States, Canada, Europe, Japan and China. Ella is a pioneer and leader in the field of women's issues, women's studies, and innovative management. She is also known across the world as a motivator, educator and one of the most knowledgeable teachers in the area of personal success and self-esteem.

She is President of Knowledge Concepts Publishing; Publisher and Editor-in-chief of Global One Magazine and CEO of Sexy Girl Apparel. Ella Patterson is available for media interviews, book signings and speaking engagements.

She lives outside Dallas Texas with her husband.

Ella can be reached at
Email: ellampatterson@aol.com
Telephone: Call 972-854-1824
Website: http://www.ellapattersonbooks.com
Twitter: Tweet me your comments @emp55

Books, Audiotapes, Videos

By Ella Patterson

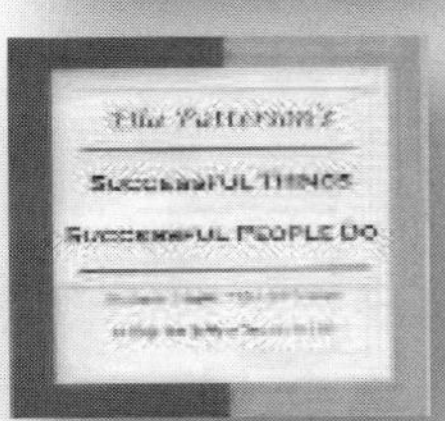

At Knowledge Concepts Publishing

Our Mission

Encourage women through our publications to explore life's benefits without apology.

Our Vision

Empower and educate women so that they can experience strong and healthy mindsets leading to a positive impact not only in their relationships, but also in their lives.

Our Goal

Make it easy and fun for women to tap into a part of themselves that gives confidence and higher levels of self-esteem.

A Moving Thought

Always be a first rate version of yourself instead of a second rate version of somebody else.

\- Judy Garland

Order Form

☐ YES, I want ________ copies of Moving in the book. All orders must be accompanied with payment of $14.95 each in the form of a money order in U.S. funds before shipment. Books cannot be sent without proper payment and postage. Please allow 15 days for delivery.

Name: ____

Address: ____

City: ____________ State: ______________ Zip: ____________

Telephone Number (_________) ______________________

Ship To: (fill in only if different from mailing address)

Name: ____

Title: ____

Address: ____

City: ____

Telephone Number (_________) ______________________

Signature: ____

Thank You!

Mail Payment to:
Knowledge Concepts Publishing
Book: Moving in the Right Direction
P.O. Box 973
Cedar Hill, Texas 75104

The world as we have created it is a process of our thinking.
It cannot be changed without changing our thinking.

\- Albert Einstein